Deadbeat Dad

CLARK KENT

Deadbeat Dad © 2017 by Clark Kent

All rights reserved. Printed in the United States of America. No part of this book may be used or reproduced in any manner whatsoever without written permission except in the case of brief quotations embodied in critical articles or reviews.

This book is a work of partial non-fiction. However, names, characters, businesses, organizations, places, events and incidents either are the product of the author's imagination or are used fictitiously. Any resemblance to actual persons, living or dead, events, or locales is entirely coincidental.

For information contact: info@uptownmediaventures.com

Book and Cover design by Team Uptown

ISBN: 978-1-68121-057-5

First Edition: February, 2017

10 9 8 7 6 5 4 3 2 1

Dedication

Dedicated to all the alienated fathers around the world.

Page intentionally left blank

Table of Contents

Introduction		7
1	The Lonely Old Man	13
2	Stepmom	25
3	The Little Sponges Called Four Year Olds	31
4	Jungle Fever	39
5	Proof	47
6	Hunters and Game	53
7	Black Like Me	61
8	Lovers and Friends	67
9	Crash	77
10	Nightmares	83
11	Back to Business	87
12	Baby Girl	95
13	Star Struck	105
14	The Girls	117
About the Author		125

Page intentionally left blank

Introduction

I would like to explain to you the origin of the term *"Baby Daddy."* During the 1990's only 3 out of 10 black babies born were conceived by married couples. Of those children only 1 out of 100 would be raised by couples who stayed together. It basically became common place for young black couples to make babies with no intention on raising those children in what we know as a family. As a result the black family unit became almost non-existent. The fathers of these babies born out of wedlock were disassociated from these unmarried families and were called "baby daddies."

The mothers of these children were referred to likewise as "Baby mommas." These titles were in no way meant as terms of endearment. It was just another way of mentally separating black and other low income couples and dividing families. It served as a reminder that these young couples were not meant to be the makers of families.

Nobody stays single forever though. It is said that there is somebody for everybody. Life goes on and eventually new relationships begin and families are rebuilt. As they say one man's trash is another man's treasure. A broken family can be repaired by a single mother or father by starting a new relationship. It's like a ready-made family - *"Just add Dad."*

CLARK KENT

Many men stepped in and began to raise the families left behind by other men who became victims of the rise of gangs and the crack epidemic. It seemed like the perfect compromise. A man who for whatever reason couldn't be there to watch his children grow up could fill the void of his lost family by helping a single mother raise her kids. The truth is that in most cases as sad as it sounds some of these men did better with the ready-made family than they could have ever done with the family they had started.

It is proof of two things that are the main reasons why it is not supposed to be okay to have children out of wedlock. First of all just because a man and a woman make a baby together doesn't mean that they are compatible enough to raise that child together. Second of all, a woman and her children need someone to take the role of father in order to survive. Hence the term *"Just add Dad."*

Of course there are exceptions to every rule. There are many women who some way or another raise their children without help from anyone. Well almost without help from anyone, some women find the help from good old' Uncle Sam.

A woman who has children gets to claim those children on her taxes, and receive earned income credit on her taxes. The government gives her thousands of dollars every year even if they have received child support throughout the year. On top of that they will help her track down her baby's daddy and force him to pay child support.

Deadbeat Dad

Of course not every mother gets the child support that is due to her. Some men slip through the cracks and get away with not ever paying child support. On the other hand there are many men who get child support taken from every check that they earn even though they don't get to be a part of their children's lives. The child support system can take up to 65% of a father's income.

When tax time comes and that father goes to do his taxes he first finds out that there is no government tax relief for him. The money that has been taken out of his check for child support is not taxable and there is no tax break for fathers who pay their child support. He also finds that if he is behind on his child support his income tax return gets taken.

His neighbor is a single mother with three children. Her rent is paid by section 8, food stamps provide all of their food, she gets money from child support and on top of that she just got her taxes back and bought a nice car. They have been talking to each other occasionally in passing.

Today she is looking really good. As he walks up to his apartment building she is unloading the groceries from the car. He stops to help her and she is very appreciative. It sparks the beginning of a new relationship. As they say "opposites attract."

They start to spend time together, and she sees that he is really good with her children. Eventually they hook up and sooner or later they decide that he should move in. He can barely pay his bills after the child support comes out of his check. To him it's a win/win situation. One woman's deadbeat dad becomes another

CLARK KENT

woman's step in dad of the year. Everybody wins. The kids get a male role model, the mother gets a new man, and the man gets a new family.

When a couple breaks up the child naturally stays with the mother. The father has to start all over. He may be lucky enough to still have visitation but he no longer has the chance to live with his children. Most times after the split up, the mother uses the child as a way to control the father.

He has to play whatever game she chooses to use on him if he wants to see the child. The father eventually gets tired of being used. Some fathers go to court to get court ordered visitation. Other fathers just give up and pray that one day they will be able to reunite with the child or children.

The mother on the other hand, is still able to have a family. Of course I'm not taking away the fact that it is almost impossible sometimes to keep up with the duty of being a single parent. The truth of the matter however; is that she gets to continue to see her children every day. She never has to wonder if her children are thinking about her because the children still live with her even though things didn't work out between the "mommy and daddy." Everything will be ok; all she has to do is add a new dad.

We see it every day. A man meets a single mom; they start dating and the next thing you know he has moved in and the kids are calling him Daddy. It's not his fault any more than her or the children's. A void has been left and needs to be filled.

Deadbeat Dad

In reality he most likely has children of his own that for whatever reason he is separated from. He is doing the same thing that the mother and the children are doing; trying to fill the void left behind by a failed relationship. It helps him to get over the pain of missing his children just being able to be there for someone else's children. You find that a child doesn't have to be biologically yours to steal your heart and mean just as much to you.

Chapter 1
The Lonely Old Man

This is the story of a lonely man. The story of how parental alienation can rip a man's heart right out of his chest. I'm 41 years old. I have 7 kids by 5 women. Today I am sitting alone. I haven't seen any of my kids in at least two years. A crazy chain of events has ripped all of my babies away from me. I accept partial responsibility, but not everything can be blamed on me.

I really can't explain how it ended up like this. All I ever wanted was to be a father. I had grown up in a house with both parents. I had always admired the way my father cherished his family. Of course my parents had some fights and arguments, but somehow they had stayed together.

I sat watching children play in the playground saddened and wondering if my kids ever thought about me. I had been there to see all of my children born, had watched each one take their first steps and even seen every one of them off on their first days of school. I missed hearing them run through the house, missed yelling at them to quiet down. They had left footprints on my heart and soul yet here I am alone with only memories.

I guess that's why I liked to sit in the park. It was a way to enjoy watching young children enjoy themselves. The sound of their laughter helped to ease

CLARK KENT

the pain of missing my own children. Sometimes I would sit and daydream about times I had spent with my babies. Now some of them were grown or almost grown, I was missing the chance to see them blossom into the wonderful young adults they were becoming.

My oldest son was fifteen when I found out that I wasn't his biological father. It was too late for it to even matter anymore. We had grown together over the years and nothing would ever be able to break that bond. I was and still am his father.

I will never forget the pain that I felt when his grandmother showed up to take him away. We had lived together all summer. When I asked his grandmother to get his things ready for me to enroll him into the school, she procrastinated and always had an excuse why she hadn't brought the things that I needed to enroll him in school. I knew something was wrong.

His mother had given up custody of him to her mother when he was born. We were young, still basically kids ourselves. She was suffering from severe postpartum depression and at the age of sixteen she wasn't ready for a baby. She hated that I had gotten her pregnant and ruined her body as well as her life.

I had made up my mind. I was going to do whatever it took to be in my son's life. School wasn't important to me at the time. All I wanted to do was get a job so I would be able to provide for my son. Every Friday I was going to be there to pick him up.

Every Friday his mother would have her hand out for money. I had promised to give her $100 every payday,

Deadbeat Dad

and she made sure that she was around to collect. Some Fridays she would show up at my job while I was still working. If for some reason I didn't have her money she was sure to raise hell.

Usually I would show up with diapers, toys, and an outfit or two. Eventually I started taking him to my house on the weekends. She would give me the same speech every time. *"Don't have my baby around any of your little bitches. Don't smoke around him, and make sure you call my mother before you bring him home."* I knew the speech by heart.

As I would be putting him in his stroller she would bat her eyes at me and ask if I could give her a little more money. At first I would give in and give her an extra twenty or so just to keep her from tripping out but she was never satisfied. Each time she wanted more and more money.

I used to love walking through the neighborhood with my newborn baby in his stroller. He was a summer baby born on July 6th. As we walked people would wave from their porches. I could usually hear people commenting on what I great father I was. I was proud to be there for my son. I refused to be like the "baby daddy's" who didn't take care of their children.

I was eighteen years old, and I was being a man. I had everything that he needed at my house. He had a crib, a swing, a playpen, even toys that he was too young to play with. I had onesies, and bibs, sleepers, and diapers, as well as bottles and formula.

I had always wanted to be a father. I loved the fact that I had a baby boy. I had learned how to make his bottles

CLARK KENT

before he was even born. I knew how to change his diapers, I even knew when he needed his diaper changed before he even started to cry. At night I slept lightly if at all when he was with me. As soon as he started to cry in the middle of the night I was right there ready with a bottle and a new diaper.

When he was old enough to crawl, I would put him on a blanket in the middle of the floor and play with him. I loved hearing him make noises and laugh. He was a happy baby. If he was crying it was only because he needed to be burped, or had gotten bored. I had his schedules down packed.

My parents were proud of how good a father I had become. My mother always smiled as she watched me play with him. We were inseparable. I had him from Friday until Sunday every week. There was nothing in the world that would keep me away from him. During the week I even went to see him even though I knew his grandmother wouldn't let me take him. Sometimes it seemed like she was jealous of our relationship.

I was the first of my friends to become a father. My friends would call me on the weekends and ask if I wanted to hang out, but I always declined. I didn't feel like a teenager anymore. My son's mother was the total opposite. She spent her weekends partying with her girlfriends, spending the money I had given her on clothes for herself, and partying with her friends.

My son loved when I put him in his stroller and took him for walks. As we would walk through the neighborhood he would sit looking at everything we went past. Girls would often flirt with me when they saw us out walking. I would occasionally flirt back with some of them. I loved the attention that came with being "a good father".

His first pair of shoes was a pair of Jordan's. He was still too young for hard bottom shoes; he hadn't even begun to walk. I told myself that he would always have the best of everything. I worked hard to make sure that he did.

As he got older his mother began spending time with him. She had gotten over her postpartum depression and wanted to be a mother again. Some weekends I would go to pick him up only to find that his mother had beaten me to the punch. Of course she would show up at my job on payday for her weekly spending money. She always had an excuse why she needed more money, but never told me when she was going to take him for the weekend. Eventually I started dodging her on payday.

The first time that I called with an excuse why I wouldn't be giving her any money that week was when I saw just how evil and devious she could be. I was working in a heating and cooling warehouse. I had taken lunch early to avoid seeing her. I decided that if she was going to play games with my visiting time, I would play games with the money she had become accustomed to getting.

She was standing outside by my car when I got off of work. I had left her a message saying that I wouldn't be able to give her any money until my next payday. She was pissed. As soon as I walked out of the door of my job she started yelling. She called me every dirty name

CLARK KENT

in the book. She had planned to make a scene, and was doing one hell of a job doing it.

She stood by the driver's side door of my car and refused to move until I gave her *"her money"*. I had never seen her so upset. As I walked to the car she got even louder. My boss came to the dock to see what the commotion was. When he saw what was going on he told her she had to leave.

She turned her rage on him. She called him every kind of white motherfucker she could think of. I thought he was going to fire me. When he threatened to call the police she kicked my car and jumped into her car, peeling rubber as she pulled out of the parking lot. She didn't go far. She parked her car across the street from my job and waited for me to pull off.

As soon as I turned onto the street she burned rubber again doing a u turn and sped up behind my car. I thought she was going to crash into me as I stopped at the light. She jumped out of her car and started coming towards me yelling at the top of her lungs. I stepped on the gas and ran through the light to get away from her.

The car chase continued until I pulled up in front of her mother's house. She had almost run into my car a few times on the way. All the time she was blowing her horn and yelling out of her window at me. As I was getting out of the car she almost ran me over pulling into the driveway. She jumped out of her car and ran for the front porch. She opened the door and slammed it behind her before I could get to the first step.

Her mother came to the door looking almost as mad as she was. She asked me to leave and told me that I

Deadbeat Dad

wouldn't be taking him that weekend. I was furious. How could they be doing this to me? I had given her money every payday up until now and had never complained. She was treating me like some kind of deadbeat dad.

She had called and apologized a few days before my next payday, and invited me to come and spend some time with her and my son. I knew she was just trying to make sure that I would have her money, but I went along with it anyway. I showed up with diapers and formula for him, and some money for her. I didn't want anything to keep me from seeing my boy.

Things seemed to be going good again. It had been months since the day that she had decided to show her mean streak. As long as she got her money there was no problem. My son was turning one year old and was starting to walk. His mother had moved into her own apartment and we were rotating weekends with him. I didn't like the arrangement but there was nothing I could do about it.

On his first birthday I had asked if I could take him for the weekend with my family on a camping trip. I had been planning on his birthday for weeks. On the day that I was supposed to pick him up I took off work early. It was a Friday, but it wasn't payday so his mother hadn't showed up at my job.

I called his grandmother's house from work just before quitting time and got no answer. I called his mother and once again didn't get an answer. When I had asked her the week before, his mother had promised that she would let me take him. She had even smiled and kissed me when I gave her the money. Now as I left my job I knew that I had been played.

I drove to his grandmother's house, but no one was there. I drove to his mother's apartment building and no one answered her door. I had bought presents, and a birthday cake. I had even packed everything that he needed for the trip the night before. I had talked to his grandmother who had told me that I could take him for the weekend, but now I couldn't find them. I went on the camping trip anyway. It was a sad weekend.

I was so mad that I started avoiding my son's mother. It had been almost a month since my son's first birthday. His mother had left me messages saying that she was going to take me to child support court if I didn't give her the money that she had gotten used to. Although it had been painful I hadn't gone to see my son. I couldn't take it anymore. I was at work on a Friday afternoon, payday of course when she showed up at my job again.

My boss had already written me up about her making scenes at the job, and I had told her that if she came to my job I would not see her. I was pulling an order and putting it on the dock when I noticed her car. As I turned to go back into the warehouse I heard the horn. Before I could reach the doors to the warehouse she was out of her car carrying our baby.

A coworker of mine was standing on the dock as she walked up the stairs to where I was standing. I thought she was about to make a scene but instead she called my name in a low voice. I turned and saw her standing there not saying a word. At first I wanted to ignore her

Deadbeat Dad

and go inside, but when I saw my son I immediately changed my mind.

It had only been a month since I had last seen him but he looked much bigger. When I reached for him his eyes lit up and he started smiling. She handed him to me and watched as I kissed him and told him how much I had missed him. My coworker walked over to see the baby.

"He's adorable," she said as she leaned over to see him. "How old is he?" she asked.

"He just turned a year old," I said as I handed him back to his mother.

"We need to talk," his mother said as she put him back into his carrier.

I knew what she wanted, but I didn't want to hear it.

"I get off at four," I said as I lit a cigarette.

"Can we talk then," she asked.

"That depends, when can I have him for the weekend?" I asked.

"Look! I know you're still mad about his birthday, but it doesn't have to be like this. He needs his father," she said. "Come to my house when you get off of work please?"

I didn't want her to start going crazy again so I agreed. When I went back inside I asked my boss to let me leave early. I explained to him what was going on and he let me leave two hours early. I went home and picked up my son's birthday gifts, changed clothes and headed over to see my son.

CLARK KENT

When I got to her house she had the lights low and candles burning in the living room. As I walked in the door I could smell food cooking. I walked in and sat on the couch. It was still daylight but she had the curtains closed and the apartment was dark.

She came into the living room carrying my son and sat beside me. He was asleep and she laid him on the far end of the couch. We hadn't been intimate since before he was born. I knew she had a trick up her sleeve. She was wearing a short dress and had her hair braided. She looked good but I really had no interest in her.

"I know you're mad, but I want to make it up to you," she said as she kissed me. I couldn't resist her. The next thing I knew we were making love. When we were finished we stood on her balcony smoking cigarettes. She apologized again and I fell for it. When she asked me for her money I gave it to her, feeling like I had just paid for sex.

She wasn't that great of a cook. Her idea of a home cooked meal was Stouffer's lasagna and garlic bread. As we ate I looked at my son still fast asleep on the couch and thought about how much I had missed him. I had actually hurt myself more than I had hurt her by staying away.

That weekend I took my son to the zoo. He was still too young to know what was going on, but I enjoyed it. I hadn't been to the zoo since I was a kid. Every time we got to another cage I picked him up so he could see the animals. The monkey cage really caught his attention. The monkeys came right up to the cage as we stood there. He looked at the cage with wide eyes. He didn't look scared at all. We watched as the monkeys swung from tree to tree.

As we were walking past the giraffes I saw a beautiful girl with a young kid looking at the giraffes. As I walked past she saw me looking, so I had to speak. After talking to her for a while I found out that the kid was her younger brother. She was eighteen, and had just moved to the city. We exchanged phone numbers and I told her I would call her. As she walked away I looked back at her sexy body and knew I'd be calling her that night.

After we left the zoo we went to my parent's house for dinner. My parents had moved into a new house and left their two bedroom apartment to me. It was the first time that I had seen them since they had moved. When my mother opened the door she immediately grabbed my son.

My father was in the living room watching the news as I walked in. The city had been having problems with the local gangs. The news reporter was talking about how the murder rate had doubled since the year before. The police were putting together a gang task force to deal with the problem. My father turned off the television and stood to greet me.

"How's my grandbaby," he asked as I sat on one of the recliners.

"He's doing pretty good. Mama took him as soon as we walked in. We went to the zoo today. I think he liked it," I told him as he sat back on the couch. We sat talking for a while as he smoked a joint. My father had always liked his weed, and he wasn't ashamed to say so.

CLARK KENT

He asked how work was going and if I needed anything for my apartment. I told him everything was fine and that I had converted one of the bedrooms into a nursery and play room for my son. He told me that he had bought some toys for him and had been waiting for me to bring him over.

I told him about my visit with my son's mother but left out the part about us making love. I told him that we had made up and that things were okay for the moment. As we were talking I wondered if he had gone through the same kind of craziness with his first wife about seeing the kids. He and my mother had been married since before me or any of my siblings were born so I knew my mom hadn't played games about seeing the kids.

I wanted to ask him but I knew that he didn't like talking about his ex-wife, so I kept my questions to myself. My mother came in and handed my son to my father. As I watched them play I thought about all of the fun he must've had with us as babies. I had to admit that he had gotten off easy. My father had never changed a diaper, because that was a job for Mama.

Chapter 2
Stepmom

My son's mother hadn't changed at all, if anything she had gotten worse. We had drifted apart and I really didn't see her that much. Usually her mother would bring him to my house on the weekends that he wasn't with his mom, which was becoming more and more often. I had started dating the girl I had met at the zoo.

Her name was Angie. She was a waitress at Baker's Square, a restaurant that was not far from my house. Occasionally she would come to my apartment and spend the night after work. We had gotten really close. She knew that I had a son, but other than the time at the zoo she had never been around him. His mother had made a point of always warning me about having chicks around my son.

My son was two years old and he was a handful. He was walking, and talking and getting into everything that he could. One night while he was there Angie came to see me. When she called and told me that she was on her way I almost asked if she could come another time. After giving it half a thought, I told her that she could come over and watch The Lion King with me and my son.

At first my son was shy. He hid behind my legs when she came into the living room. She had skills with kids though and they were laughing and playing in no time.

CLARK KENT

We watched the movie, even though my son only made it halfway through. I knew the movie by heart; it was his favorite and mine too.

After the movie she carried him to his bedroom and laid him down to sleep. She stood there looking at him. I could tell that she really loved kids. When she came back into the living room she had tears in her eyes. I wondered why she was crying but didn't want to pry. Later that night she told me that she had gotten a back alley abortion when she was sixteen, and wasn't able to have kids.

I had heard the term "back alley abortion", but really didn't know much about it. The way she made it sound brought chills to my spine. It sounded like something that no human being should have to go through.

As time went by it became a natural thing to have Angie over when my son was there. They got along really good. We took him to parks and I watched as they fed the ducks. At night she would give him his bath and put him to sleep. It was really a big help having her around. She absolutely adored him.

Our relationship had gotten deeper and deeper. Eventually I asked her to move in with me. I wanted her there full time. She was a great cook, and I really liked spending time with her. So did my son.

We always did fun things on the weekends. It was almost like being a real family. She did everything for him that a caring mother would do. Her only rule was that he had to call her by her name. She made it a point to ask him how his mommy was when he came over. She said that she would never try to take the place of his mother. The funny thing was that she probably had been spending twice as much time with him as his real mother.

One weekend his mother picked him up from his grandmother's house early that Friday morning. She had come to my job just as I was getting off of work. When I walked out to my car there she was. As soon as she saw me she started yelling at me.

"Nigga you know you need to give me my child support money now!" The closer I got to the car the louder she screamed. "I take care of our son! I'm the one that buys his clothes. You need to be a man and stop avoiding me," she yelled as I reached the front of the car. By now other people who worked in the warehouse were coming out of the building.

"What is your problem? Are you trying to get me fired?" I asked.

"You haven't given me money in over a month," She yelled.

"You haven't had him in over a month. If anything I should be giving my money to your mama. She's the one who takes care of him while you run the streets chasing every dope boy you can find," I yelled as I pushed her away from my car. I unlocked my car and opened the door.

"That's a lie! He isn't even with my mama. He's at my house and if you want to see him you better have my money," she yelled as I got in and closed my door. I started the car and gave her the finger. As I pulled away

CLARK KENT

she hit my back windshield with a rock. The windshield broke with a loud crash.

I slammed on the brakes and stopped the car. I opened my door and was almost run over as the car she was in burned rubber and took off out of the parking lot. She was hanging out of the passenger side of the car yelling at the top of her lungs.

I got back into my car and pulled off. It was the middle of the winter and I was driving with a busted back window. I had had enough of her bullshit. I promised myself that I would never speak to her again.

That night at about ten o clock, my phone started ringing. I answered the phone to see who it was.

"Hello."

"Your son is tripping," said a voice on the other end of the phone.

"Who is this?" I asked as I reached for the caller I.D. box.

"It's yo baby mama, who else you have calling you this late while my son is there?" she replied

"You trippin, he ain't here and you know it. Besides what business is it of yours who calls me? I ain't got nothing to do with you," I said

"Look, I'm not even calling for all that," she replied. "I was just calling because he won't stop crying. He keeps saying that he wants his "anzy." What is that, some kind of toy or something?" I almost broke out laughing. He was asking for *His Angie.* I was glad that she didn't know what he was really saying. I thought it was kind of funny and messed up that he was with his mother and asking to be with Angie.

I told her that I didn't know what an anzy was. I told her to ask her mother if she knew what it was. It was my way of letting her know that she was never around enough to be able to understand what he was saying. I hung up the phone and put it back in its cradle. When I told Angie we both laughed.

The saddest thing about bringing people into your children's lives is that eventually you may have to explain to your children why the person they grew to love is gone. Not gone as in dead but gone as in "Daddy just had to let her go."

My son was almost three when Angie and I broke up. He yearned for her more than he did for his own mother. How was I supposed to make it sound good to a two year old? Should I sit him down and say "Look son I know you miss her but she messed with Daddy's friend and she won't be coming back... Don't worry though I'll get you a new one." Of course not, I did what any Dad would do. I told him that she had gone out of town. I told him that she would be back some day. Eventually he stopped asking about her.

Chapter 3
The Little Sponges Called Four Year Olds

By the time my son was four years old he knew everything. He could sing the ABC song at the drop of a hat. He knew his colors, his shapes; he could even count to twenty, if you gave him credit for the few numbers that he occasionally left out. He also learned things that he wasn't supposed to learn. He saw everything and nothing got past him.

Every time that it was our weekend he would say something else that would blow my mind. He came up with some of the most shocking questions too. He was a sponge, and he absorbed everything he saw or heard. Sometimes I would think that I had gotten something past him, only to be questioned about it later. They say that smart children ask questions and my son didn't miss a beat.

One day we were sitting on our balcony and he was playing with his new fire truck. He turned to me out of nowhere and asked, "Daddy why do boys have nipples?" I didn't know what to say. I looked at him laughing and asked why he would ask me such a question. "Because momma said the reason girls have nipples is to feed the babies. Who do we feed Daddy?" he asked. I couldn't believe that a four year old would be thinking of something like that.

CLARK KENT

"I don't know little man. I guess we'll find out one day," I said as I sat looking at him. He shrugged it off and started back playing with his new fire truck as if he had never asked the question. I wondered what he was thinking of now.

I kept my son in new clothes everywhere we went. He always had on a new pair of Michael Jordan basketball shoes and usually he had a Jordan t-shirt to match. He wasn't like a lot of other kids his age. He didn't like getting dirty. At the playground he usually stuck to the swings. Every once in a while he would venture to the sliding board but that was as far as he went.

I always made sure he had snacks for the park. Hot Cheetos were his favorite. He would always come for his snacks with a new friend. I'd give him the snacks and he would run off to share them with every kid on the playground. He was always able to make friends.

One day while we were at the park I noticed that he didn't want to play. The usual kids were there but he wasn't into it. I sat at my regular picnic table next to the park and opened our bag. We had sodas and chips. I had a beer.

I didn't push it but as he sat there quietly, looking at the playground, I wondered what was on his little mind. When he didn't respond to me putting the snacks on the table I had to ask. "Boy why aren't you playing?" He turned around and looked at me with his most serious face.

"Daddy, why don't you and mommy live together?" he asked as he folded his hands on the table. It occurred to me that he had never seen his mommy and me as a couple. We had broken up right before I had found out she was pregnant. She and I were like fire and water, and we just didn't work out.

I was in shock once again. I had never had to answer a question like that from him. He was four years old and was able to understand that his mother and I had never lived together. He sat looking at me as if he really demanded an answer. He was serious and I knew this one wouldn't blow over without a proper response.

I broke it down to him the best way I could without saying too much. He sat listening as if he understood exactly what I was saying. His serious face turned into his curious face.

"I member Angie was your girlfriend. Why did she go out of town Daddy? Did you make her mad like you do when mommy says bad words to you?" he asked.

"Little man we're at the playground. You should be playing not asking grown up questions. Go have some fun," I told him. He grabbed a bag of his hot Cheetos and walked off to the playground. Like I said he was a sponge and nothing got past him.

After the incident with Angie I had learned my lesson. I had promised myself that I would keep my girlfriends away from my son. I knew that he had gotten attached to her and I also saw how much he missed her. His mother never found out what his anzy was, but I knew. Every time he came to my house he would run to the room to see if she was there. It hurt me to know that he had gotten hurt over our break up. He seemed to know that there was more to it than her just going out of town and never coming back.

CLARK KENT

One Friday evening in the early spring we went to visit my parents. Their house was in a cul-de-sac in Bedford heights. The street was filled with families. Everybody knew everything about everybody. Everybody in the cul-de-sac was like a family.

As soon as my son and I got out of the car my son took off running in the direction of the picnic area and playground. There were two picnic tables under a hut next to a small playground where the people of the cul-de-sac congregated. It had a great view of the sunset and was my father's favorite hangout.

As my son ran across the grass he yelled "Paw Paw! Paw Paw! Paw Paw Pawwwww!" My father got up from his seat and ran towards my son. He picked him up and swung him around in the air. They loved each other.

"How's my little man?" my father asked him.

"Good," he replied." I walked over to the table where a few of my parent friends were sitting around drinking beers. I knew most of the neighbors but there were a few people I didn't know. One of the neighbors, an older Puerto Rican man named Antonio, opened a blue cooler and handed me a beer.

"Happy Friday to you," he said as I sat down. My father and my son walked over and stood next to the table. As soon as my father put my son down he took off to the playground. My father pulled a joint out of his pocket and lit it as he watched my son run to the playground.

I opened my beer as I watched my son stop by the swings. Two little girls were swinging on the swings.

Deadbeat Dad

My son stood there talking to the girls. Eventually one of the girls jumped from her swing and walked towards the slide. My son looked like he was having problems deciding whether he wanted to hop on the swing or follow the little girl to the slide. He chose the swings, his all-time favorite playground feature.

I noticed that I was being watched. I could feel it. At the table across from where we sat there were three people. Two of them I recognized. They were the young couple who lived across from my parents. But the chick, who was staring at me, was someone I had never met. She was an older white chick. She looked to be in her late twenty's. I nodded in her direction and raised my beer. She waved and raised her beer smiling at me.

I sat talking to my father and Antonio, smoking a joint and drinking my beer. Every once in a while I would look up and see her staring at me. Antonio was talking about baseball. He was telling us that the Cleveland Indians were looking good. He spat out stats and talked about rosters. He was one of those people who just didn't shut up when he got started about sports.

After I finished my beer I called for my son. It was getting dark and he needed to be inside. We walked past the picnic tables and I told my father that I would be right back out. Antonio staggered over to the table that the white girl and the couple were sitting at. He was good and drunk. I could hear him singing sounding as if someone was killing a cat. He was singing "Walk this way," by The Rolling Stones, and doing a terrible job of it.

CLARK KENT

As I got to my parents' house I looked back at the tables. Everybody was laughing and talking. I was still being checked out by the white girl. It was as if she were a cat looking at a canary I had to be careful because she looked as if she would pounce at any time.

When we got inside Mama was sitting in the living room with a jacket on her lap. She had her embroidery hoops clamped to it and was doing a beautiful picture in her embroidery thread. She put the jacket aside and picked up my son.

"Hey Nana," my son said as he kissed her cheek.

"How's Nana's baby?" She asked as she sat down in her chair with him. He knew exactly what was up. He knew that she had a surprise for him in the bag next to her chair.

"Nana what's in your bag?" he asked looking excited.

"I don't know… Why would there be something in my bag?" she asked being silly.

"Because I been good Nana! Because I'm Nana's big boy," he said giggling with his hands around her neck. She reached over and opened her bag. He leaned with her as she pulled out a new football for him.

"Thank you Nana! Look Dad, I got a football," he said as she handed it to him. "Is that all nana?" he asked still smiling from ear to ear. She sat him on the ground and picked up her bag. She pretended to be rummaging around in it.

"Let's see… I don't know if there's anything else in there. Have you really been a good boy?" she asked.

Deadbeat Dad

"Yes Nana I been a really, really good boy," he said as he tossed the ball in the air and caught it. She pulled out a small hanger with Lion King Pajamas. His eyes got big and he jumped back into her lap. "Simba!" he yelled as he hugged the pajamas. I gave my mother a kiss and went to the kitchen to see what she had cooked. I had the munchies and I was feeling the joint I had hit.

After making myself a sandwich I walked back into the Living room. My mother had taken my son upstairs for a bath. I ate my sandwich and headed back out to the picnic tables. I could hear rap music as I approached. There must've been some sort of cul-de-sac curfew or something because the crowd had changed. The mothers and children had gone in. At the tabled now there were more people. Most of them were men. A few young couples had joined the party as well.

My father was talking to Antonio at the far end of the table. Two of the younger guys were rapping. A few people were standing in a circle around them listening to the guys rap. I looked around and saw that the chick that had been checking me out was gone. I grabbed a beer from the cooler and sat by my father.

"Boy you better watch out! I saw the way Tammy was looking at you. That girl is something else. You better watch out," Antonio said as I sat down. My father passed me a joint and laughed as he exhaled the smoke from the joint.

"That boy doesn't want anything to do with that! He has enough drama with his baby's momma. I heard about what she did at your job," my father said. He knew some of the contractors who bought their

CLARK KENT

supplies at my job. Rumors spread quickly especially at work.

"Yeah that girl is a trip. She almost got me fired, and she ain't even my girlfriend," I said as I handed Antonio the joint.

"Welcome to it young man. All of em' is crazy," Antonio said as he took a long pull from the joint. My father stood up and told us he was going inside. I sat talking to Antonio for a while. By the time he headed inside I was standing in the circle rapping with the boys who had been rapping earlier.

We rapped for a while but these guys really sucked at it. After the rap session went around twice it was plain to see that they just weren't on my level. I had been rapping for years and was really good at free styling.

The group of people who had been standing around listening had migrated back to the tables. I walked over to the cooler and grabbed another beer. As I opened it I sat at the table listening to the conversation. They were talking about Tammy. Apparently she had kicked her ex out just the week before. Now I knew why she had been staring at me with those hungry blue eyes. She was looking for a replacement.

Chapter 4
Jungle Fever

One night I was hanging out at the picnic tables at my parent's house. It was a Saturday night and I had my son with me. When he got sleepy he went into my parent's house and went to sleep. There had been some drama in the cul-de-sac earlier that evening and everybody had gone in early.

I rolled a blunt of some really good weed I had gotten from the drive- thru spot where weed dealers ran up to your car at the stop light and competed to see who would make the sale. There were always good deals on weed there. I was alone at the picnic benches that night because of whatever confrontation between nosey neighbors had happened earlier.

My parents had taken my son to the carnival that day so they were clueless about what had transpired. We pulled into the cul-de-sac at the same time and the first thing any of us noticed was that there was no one at the picnic tables. My parents were tired and so was my son. I picked him up from his car seat and carried him inside.

After my parents put my son to bed, they turned in too. I was bored so I decided to enjoy being alone at the picnic tables. I looked at my watch; it was almost ten o' clock. One of the neighbors looked out of his window. When he saw me at the benches he came out to tell me about the drama.

CLARK KENT

He told me that there had been a fight between two of the families of neighbors. It had started during a barbeque they were having earlier that day. Two guys had gotten into an argument over a girl. The fight got more intense and different family members became involved. By the end of the barbeque two people had been stabbed, and another person was shot. The police had come and arrested one of the guys and the families were at war.

In this cul-de-sac everybody had always seemed like family. These people hung out every afternoon and kicked it through the evenings. Occasionally someone would get a little too drunk and cause a scene, but there was never even as much as a fight in this neighborhood. The incident had really affected the cul-de sac.

As we were smoking the blunt, Tammy walked up. She had been drinking and from the looks of her she had been in on the drama too. The guy I had been smoking the blunt with got up and walked away as soon as he saw her coming. She walked over and sat down on the bench facing away from me.

I didn't want to bother her but I was curious about the drama. After a moment of awkward silence I asked if she was alright. She started crying and put her head down on the table. Whatever had gone down she didn't want to talk about it. I finished my blunt and was about to leave when I heard her voice.

"Don't go…. Can you please sit out here with me? I have more beers if you want one," she said as I turned around. I sat back down at the table next to her. Her makeup had run down her cheek from her eyes. It formed the tracks of many tears. She sat up and wiped her face. "I'll be back I'm going to go get those beers, she said as she walked away. It was going to be the first time that I had been alone with her since I had noticed her checking me out.

She came back out in a short dress with sandals on. She was carrying a six pack of Budweiser beer, smiling as she approached the picnic tables. She had redone her makeup and was looking like she was going on a date. Whatever had been bothering her earlier was far from her mind.

She sat on the opposite side of the table from me and handed me a beer. She pulled out a pack of cigarettes and sat them on the table. I opened my beer and tapped it against hers. "Cheers," I said as I took a sip. I noticed that she wasn't exactly flirting now that we were alone. I acted as if I hadn't noticed her watching me. At first we sat in silence.

She started telling me about how she had been bounced around from foster home to foster home as a kid. I sat there listening as if I were interested as she told me her life's story. By the time she was finished with the story I understood that she had definitely had a rough life. I also understood that this woman could talk your ear off.

She was twenty nine years old and a single mother, except when her baby's daddy was around which wasn't much. She told me about how jealous over her he was and that he sometimes stalked her. She said that they had been together for eight years and had recently

CLARK KENT

split up. She also told me the story about how they were directly involved in the incident from earlier.

She told me that there had been a barbeque planned for one of the families who were celebrating their anniversary. Her ex was related to one of the families from the cul-de-sac and decided to show up with his new girlfriend. Tammy had gotten jealous and made it look like she was flirting with one of the other guys who were there.

After everybody started drinking, her ex exchanged words with the guy she was flirting with. At first it was just a shouting match until the guy who she had been flirting with pulled out a knife. Her ex lunged toward him and was stabbed in his side. Another guy tried to break up the fight and was stabbed in the arm.

During the commotion her ex had pulled out a gun and started shooting at the guy who had stabbed him. Instead of hitting the guy with the knife, a bullet had hit a guy who was standing around watching. By the time the police and ambulances had arrived she said everybody was yelling at her and saying that it had all been her fault. After all of the commotion was over everybody had gone in for the night.

"So here we are," she said as she opened another beer. She opened a second one and handed it to me. "Love stinks," she said as she raised her bottle. For the rest of the night we sat talking about our failed relationships. She had war stories, and in each one she was the victim. I knew right then and there that she was bad news. I also knew that she was a white girl with a severe case of jungle fever.

Deadbeat Dad

By the time we were finished with the beers, she was sitting on my lap with her breast in my face. She asked me to ride with her to the liquor store so she could get a bottle of Hennessy. The next thing I knew, I was waking up in her bed naked. She was passed out next to me also naked holding an empty bottle of Hennessy.

I followed the trail of our clothes to the living room door. Apparently we had started stripping each other as soon as we had gotten in the house. Once I had all of my clothes I crept to the bathroom to wash up and get dressed. On my way out I looked into her bedroom and saw that she hadn't budged. I crept out quietly. It was a night I would regret for years to come.

After that night I didn't see again until a few weeks later. She was back with her ex; who was out on bail awaiting trial. I was visiting my parents when I saw them. My father and I were sitting at the picnic tables talking to a few other guys when they walked up.

He looked like Treach from the rap group Naughty by Nature. He was dark skinned with a constant scowl on his face. He was one of those guys who looked like he spent too much time doing bench presses and pushups. Right away I noticed how arrogant he was.

He was loud and always seemed to be looking for attention. He was one of those older guys who liked to talk about young chicks when his girl wasn't around. Listening to him talk made me remember some of the things his girlfriend had told me about him the night we had gotten drunk together.

She was drunk and couldn't stop talking about her baby's daddy. She had put his business out there as we

CLARK KENT

polished off the bottle of Hennessy. He was telling a story about some girls when she walked up behind him. When he noticed her at his elbow he quickly changed the subject

She whispered something in his ear and they walked off. "What a couple," I thought as they walked away. She couldn't be trusted and neither could he. I thought about the question that my son had asked me about his mother and me. The answer was that his mother and I had never really been a couple. What I had done was kept my word and always been there for him as a father.

After that day I rarely saw Tammy. I had heard that her baby's daddy was facing a lot of jail time for the shooting. When I did see her she was either getting in or getting out of her car with her daughter and occasionally her baby's daddy.

As time went on I started hanging out at my parents less and less. I was focused on my son and my job. It was the beginning of the summer and we spent our weekends at the parks, and places like the zoo, and Sea World. One day we went to The International expo center, also known as the IX center. The county fair was going on. There were rides and games, even a huge Ferris wheel.

We spent the day trying our best to ride every ride that my son was tall enough to ride. Between rides we ate junk food and cotton candy. By the time we were done for the day we were worn out. We decided to take a picture to remember the day before we left.

Deadbeat Dad

After walking around for almost another hour we found the photo booth. We stepped inside and made faces as the camera flashed. When the flashing stopped, a roll of small black and white pictures came out of the slot in the machine. I looked over at my son to show him the pictures I saw that he was fast asleep.

I folded the pictures and put them into my wallet. Once my wallet was back in my pocket I picked up my sleeping son and carried him to my car. It had been a day to remember.

Chapter 5
Proof

The first person who ever dared to try to question whether or not I was Khalyl's father was Tammy. I was hanging out at my parent's house enjoying a barbeque. Pops had his grill going, his music playing, and was halfway through a bottle of Black Velvet. Some of the other neighbors were also having a cook-out. It was the fourth of July and everybody seemed to be getting along and in a good mood.

Pops pulled a joint out of his shirt pocket and handed it to me. I could tell from looking at it that Pops had been drunk when he rolled it. The joint had a big bulge in the middle of it and the ends were twisted tight. The joint looked like it was pregnant with twins.

I lit it and inhaled the smoke of some very high end weed. Pops only smoked the best weed. I felt like I was hovering over my own body. When I hit the joint a second time my head seemed like it exploded and I couldn't stop coughing. I passed the joint back to Pops and opened a beer. As I sat there listening to the combination of The Commodores and stories of my father's past, Tammy walked up.

I hadn't seen her in quite a while. Right away I noticed that she was pregnant. She had a can of Pepsi in her hand and was wearing an oversized t-shirt and shorts. She said hello to everyone and took a seat at one of the picnic tables. I had heard that her baby's daddy had

CLARK KENT

gone to prison. All of the neighbors were back together as friends. They had let by gones be by gones.

I sat at the table next to her and said hello. She looked at me as though there was something that she wanted to tell me, but was afraid to say anything. She kind of forced a smile, which was really more of a smirk than anything else and turned her attention to the political debate going on between two of the neighbors.

Out in the street the children were in the middle of a water balloon fight. Water balloons exploded as the children chased each other laughing and playing. The summer sky had begun to change colors as the day came to an end. The city of Bedford always had a fireworks show on Independence Day. It usually started an hour after sunset.

As I sat watching the children play I noticed that Tammy had moved closer to where I was sitting. She was watching me. I turned to look at her just in time to see her staring at me with lust in her eyes.

As soon as our eyes met she turned away as if to hide the way she had been looking at me. I wondered what she was thinking about, but decided not to pry. I looked at her stomach and was reminded that she was pregnant. I got up and walked over to where my Pops and some of the other neighbors were standing passing around yet another joint.

As I reached for the joint being passed in my direction, I was plowed into by my son; who was now soaking wet. I picked him up and walked towards the picnic tables. Tammy was watching me as we sat down. I fixed our plates and put Khalyl's food in front of him.

Deadbeat Dad

"Look at you man, you're soaked! Did anybody miss you with their water balloons?" I asked.

"I think so but not really", he replied as he picked up a hot dog from the plate. "Daddy, are we going to the park to see the fireworks?" he asked as he took as big of a bite as he could.

"Yeah man, that's why you need to hurry up and eat so you can change into some dry clothes." I told him as I sipped my cold beer. As I looked at him I thought about how quickly he had grown up. Here he was at the age of five years old and able to have a semi intelligent conversation about just about anything. I wondered how he would be when he was really all grown up. I quickly shook the thought off. I told myself that I could wait until he got to the age of defiance.

"You're a great dad." Tammy said as she came and sat beside me .If you guys want you can ride with us to see the fireworks. They should be starting soon."

"Okay, I just need to get little man changed into some dry clothes. We'll be ready in about ten minutes." I said as I cleared our plates off of the table. Khalyl was already running to the house. He had been waiting for the firework show all summer. It had become a tradition for us because his birthday was July 6th.

The park was packed. People had come from all over the city to see this year's biggest and best fireworks show. Tammy found a parking space after driving around the park twice. There was a stage in the middle of the baseball field. The Cleveland Orchestra was going to play music as the fireworks were shot off. People

CLARK KENT

were gathered around the stage waiting for the show to begin.

We found a good spot on a hill to watch the show. Khalyl and Tammy's daughter sat down in the grass and we sat down behind them. The Orchestra started playing "The National anthem."

Fireworks shot off into the air, exploding in the shape of the flag of The United States. Red explosions of color filled the sky followed by blue and white as the Orchestra concluded the song and started to play another. The fireworks were exploding in sequence to the music. I was brought out of my stupor by Tammy grabbing my hand.

She pulled me close and started to kiss me. I was caught completely off guard. We pulled away from each other in an awkward silence. She was staring into my eyes like she thought I was Prince Charming.

We sat watching the rest of the firework show kind of hugging. She laid her head on my shoulder and sat staring at our children. Her daughter and my son were entranced by the colorful explosions and orchestra music. With each explosion the children looked more and more in awe.

"Are you really his father?" As soon as Tammy said it a chill went through my spine. No one had ever asked me such a question. It was as if she were purposely trying to upset me.

"Of course he is why would you say that?" I asked.

"He just doesn't look like he has a father who is not black. I mean really, look how dark he is in comparison to you," she replied in a matter of fact kind of way. "I'm sorry if it comes out in an offensive way. I'm just saying that if I were you I would've been demanding proof. Trust me; it wouldn't be the first time that somebody got tricked into believing that they were the father of a baby who they clearly were not."

We sat there in silence for what seemed to be an awkward moment. I couldn't believe that a woman who didn't even know me would make such a rude comment. And furthermore, how dare this bitch even question the paternity of my only child. I stood up, and walked to where my son was sitting, still enjoying the show.

"Let's go little man!" I said as I bent over to pick him up. The fireworks were so loud that Khalyl didn't even hear me.

"Please... Don't leave... I swear I didn't mean to offend you." Tammy said as she reached out and grabbed my arm.

"What the fuck did you mean to do then?" I asked as I pulled away. Right then the "Grand Finally" started. The music got louder and louder as fireworks exploded all over the night sky. The children roared and cheered on the show. I decided to sit back down and let my son finish watching the rest of the fireworks show. Even though I hadn't taken my son and walked off I was pissed. As I sat there I thought about the fact that she was pregnant and probably didn't really even know who the father of her baby was.

After the fireworks show I grabbed Khalyl's hand and we walked off. As we were walking I looked down at my

CLARK KENT

son. For the first time ever I was looking at him as if I were looking for signs of resemblance. I quickly shook it off and picked him up. I put him on my shoulders and we walked back to my parent's house.

After that day I didn't speak to Tammy for months. When I saw her I made sure to look in the opposite direction. I was still very upset at her for what she had said. I told Khalyl that he was not allowed to play with Tammy's daughter when we were at my parents' house. I didn't tell him why, for one thing he was too young to understand it. The other reason was because I never wanted him to have to question whether or not I was his father.

Chapter 6
Hunters and Game

Like any twenty-six year single man I was playing the field. I was dating a few different girls, but I wasn't in a relationship. I guess you could say that I had quite a few lady friends. From the outside looking in it probably looked like I was a *Mack Daddy*.

I had a girl who liked to go out, a girl who liked to stay home, a girl who liked to cook, and a girl who loved to eat in fancy restaurants, a girl who liked to buy me things, and even a girl who I liked to buy things for. Every one of them had different qualities that I really liked but I didn't view any of them as someone to settle down with. I always dealt with them squarely. I never promised anything that I didn't intend to do, and I never lied to them.

I made myself a promise that I would keep all of them away from Khalyl. I remembered how attached to Angie he was, and how bad I felt when I had to tell him that she was gone forever. I promised myself that I would never let that happen again. I had Khalyl from Friday to Sunday so that meant that I could only date during the week. The weekends belonged to us. Those days were reserved for father and son time.

Believe it or not that turned out to be the best way to meet the right women. I learned that most of the women who only went out on weekends had attachments during the week. They couldn't go out on

CLARK KENT

a spur of the moment Tuesday night because they had kids and husbands. The women who you could call during the week were usually sophisticated professional women who were very single and usually very well off.

I had met some very successful women as a result of my new dating schedule. Vicky was a Para legal. She worked for a big law firm in Parma. I usually accompanied her to events that she attended to show off for her colleagues. We were never anything like a couple. I was simply her arm candy to fend off thirsty executives.

Brenda was the manager of an apartment complex. She was a thirty year old beautiful educated black woman. She was the definition of high end. She drove a new BMW, lived in an expensive high rise condo, and only wore the most expensive clothes. She liked to stay at home drinking Chardonnay and listening to Miles Davis when she wasn't working. She liked to cook me fancy dinners. We'd sit looking over her view of the city lights and talk about politics.

And then there was Rhonda. She was my favorite. She had rich friends, and went to fancy parties. She drove fast cars and ran in circles with all of the top hustlers. She vowed to never stop being a player.

She played high stakes poker in exclusive casino's. She stayed in fancy hotels, and traveled often. She liked me to go with her when she did business because I seemed to be the only man she knew that wasn't chasing her. I liked her a lot but usually I pretended not to look at her like that. There were some intense moments but for some reason; no matter what I tried we were always just friends.

She liked to swap stories of playing the field. She had grown up the only daughter in a family of six and not only had she been spoiled but she had also been well trained in how to use men. Every one of her stories ended with her leaving with everything. She was a heartless player but she was also stunningly beautiful.

Her brothers were all pretty boy player types. They drove expensive cars and were always surrounded by sexy women. One of them had graduated from Harvard and was a lawyer. Another of them worked in some kind of marketing company. When I was around them I always felt out of place.

Her mother was the widow of an actor. She was a beautiful older black woman with expensive taste. She didn't seem happy seeing me with her daughter until she was sure we were just friends. I was definitely not the kind of guy that she would approve of her daughter being involved with. For some reason, that seemed to make Rhonda like me even more.

My playing the field caught up with me faster than I expected it to. I had been successfully playing the field for months. Even though some of the girls had caught feelings, I still hadn't committed to any of them.

All of that changed when they started calling and telling me they were pregnant. Rhonda was the first to call in pregnant. We were supposed to be going to a party at a friend of ours condo. When I went to pick her up from work, I found out that she had gone home sick.

CLARK KENT

When I finally got her on the phone she said those three words that make a man's heart skip a beat.

"Baby I'm pregnant!" I stood holding the phone in silence. I was in shock. If there ever were such a thing as bad timing; this was it. I was just beginning to get used to the single life.

"Hello! Are you there? Did you hear me?"

"Yes, I'm here. I just don't know what to say."

"Well say something! I just told you that I am having your baby."

"No! You said you were pregnant, now you're telling me you are having my baby. Don't get me wrong, I'm happy baby, just kind of caught off guard. We were just friends, now everything changes. We were both just talking about how we never wanted to be in relationships. What happens now?"

"Now life happens! We come together and raise the baby that we made. We both knew what we were doing. You can't tell me that you weren't trying to be more than friends."

I thought back to when Tammy said, "It *wouldn't be the first time that somebody got tricked into believing they were the father of a baby that they clearly were not*"

I knew that I had been a little careless. I knew that there had been times that we had been in the heat of the moment and the last thing on my mind was a condom. We talked about it for a while longer before we said goodbye. When I got off of the phone with her I sat with my head in my hands. This could change

Deadbeat Dad

everything that I was doing. This would literally turn my world upside down.

Rhonda was every man's dream, and every player's nightmare. She was half black, and half Native American. She was short and curvy with light skin and long pretty hair. Her walk made men foam at the mouth. When I met her she was reading a book in a coffee shop.

I sat at the table next to hers and ordered a coffee, black with one sugar. I wasn't much of a coffee drinker but I wanted to find a way to spark up a conversation with this beautiful exotic girl.

I opened my newspaper to the sports section and sipped my coffee reading about yet another Cavaliers loss. As I was sitting there a guy walked up to her and tried to talk to her. He was way too sure of himself, and got shot down like an enemy aircraft. When she was done with him all he could do was walk away.

When he was gone we laughed at the way he had approached her. I mimicked his cocky attitude and weak approach. We guessed that he was about forty years old with a wife and kids at home. She told me about how often she had to fight off the hounds as she called them. She was a pretty girl with a complexion like milk and the smile of a Goddess, and it was easy to imagine men going crazy over her.

From that day on we were friends. We often went out to bars or clubs together. She liked to make everyone think that we were a couple just so she could take a break from the countless advances thrown her way. She was so fine that even women were chasing her.

CLARK KENT

She was a player and that was what we had in common. She had a man for every need. Men bought her expensive things, and did whatever she told them. She knew how to play with men's minds. The thing that I learned from her was how to tell the truth to get what I wanted.

She never lied to them. She may have led them on but she never promised more than she would do for them. As a result she had a flock of men who were willing to jump at her every command. I was not one of them.

We were just friends. We enjoyed each other's company. There were never any motives between us. Now as I sat thinking of the conversation that we had just had, I knew that everything was about to change. I felt like I had fallen into her web.

I also had to think about how this would make my other lady friends feel. How could I tell them that the game was over? How could I face the fact that the hunter had been captured by the game?

The phone rang in my hand startling me back to reality. It was Brenda. I could hear the sound of the jazz that she was listening to in the background. I knew she wanted company. I looked at the clock hanging on my living room wall and saw that it was 9:00 on a Wednesday night.

She was probably wearing one of her sexy evening dresses. I could imagine how she looked standing on her balcony with a wine glass in her hand.

"What are you doing handsome?"

Deadbeat Dad

"Well I had planned to go to a friend's party but it seems as though plans have changed."

"Would you like to come over and let me make you something to eat?"

"It's a possibility, let me call you in ten minutes and let you know."

"Don't call me in ten minutes just be here in twenty!" The phone went dead. I laughed to myself as I walked out of the door. Rhonda was pregnant true enough but it was still too soon to be cutting all ties. I was on my way to be treated like a king while I still could.

By 9:30 I was standing in the lobby of Brenda's building talking to the front desk security guard. Eric was about thirty-five years old. He was the night watchmen for a luxurious high rise and he was the coolest cat in town. He knew everything about everything. The people in the building all confided in him. He was everybody's favorite ear to fill.

"My man Cool J! What's happenin' young blood? You must be headed up to see Lady Brenda huh?"

"Yeah you know me just hangin' out."

"I saw her come in here after work looking ferocious. You better be careful young blood, she's a man eater!" As he said it the phone on his desk started ringing. When he picked it up I walked over and pressed the button for the elevators. I looked back and saw Eric in *Mack Daddy* mode still on the phone. A bell rang and the elevator doors opened.

CLARK KENT

The inside of the elevator was elegantly decorated with gold trim. Mirrors on every wall gave its passengers a chance to see how well they were dressed. I pushed the button for the twenty-fifth floor and the elevator took off playing a song by Bob James. The building was made to make you feel like a part of the elite. By the time that the elevator reached her floor I was relaxed and ready to have a fancy evening.

Chapter 7
Black Like Me

I was sitting with Brenda when my phone started ringing. She had cooked me crab legs, and lobster tails. We were talking about the upcoming presidential election when I looked at my phone and saw that the call was from my parent's house. At first I ignored the call. After the third time I knew it had to be important.

Brenda was the kind of woman who saw through everything. As my phone rang she smiled and kind of gave me a chuckle. She was the woman who basically coached me on how to deal with women. I tried to focus on the remainder of the crab legs, they were perfect. As my phone began to ring for the fourth time I decided that I could no longer ignore it.

"Excuse me, I have to take this call, it's my parents," I said as I got up and walked to the balcony.

"Hello.... Who's this?"

"It's your mother! That's who! What are you doing?"

"I was having dinner. What's up Ma?"

"Did you know that Tammy had her baby?"

"No, what does that have to do with me?"

"Do you know what she named the baby?"

"No! Look Ma, it's really not a good time."

CLARK KENT

"The baby's name is Jason Jr. She's saying that you are the father of her baby!"

"What?"

"You heard me! You better get over here and talk to this woman right now! I don't know what her problem is but you better get this bullshit straightened out right now!"

The phones went dead, and for the second time in one day I stood there with my mouth open wondering how something like this could be happening to me. This was the woman who had insulted me. We had only had sex one time. We were the furthest thing from compatible that there could ever be.

I walked back inside and poured a glass of wine. I downed it immediately. I sat back at the table with Brenda. Of all of my lady friends she seemed to be the only one who I wasn't worried about getting pregnant. We weren't really romantically involved. Of course there had been times when we let ourselves get carried away but she was overly responsible when it came to safe sex. She was more like a mentor to me than anything else. She looked at me and shook her head.

"You know Jason, I worry about you. These little girls play with your heart like a toy. They have you so confused that you don't even know who you are anymore. Baby you have to harden your heart and stop being used like a puppet on a string. Be a man and stand up for your piece of mind. Don't let these bitches; who, don't even love you make you feel obligated to them." She stood up and hugged me. "I talked to Mama Sue earlier. Mama told me everything, that's why I wanted you to come here and get away from all of that nonsense. Take a deep breath and relax everything will work itself out," she said as she filled my wine glass.

I sat eating the rest of my dinner thinking about everything that was going on. It was like karma was paying me back for playing with these women's emotions. I thanked Brenda for the dinner and left to pick up my son and go to my parent's house.

It was almost 11 o'clock when I pulled onto to my parent's street. As we got out of the car I noticed that my parent's house was alive with company. My parents generally never had company this late. Something was definitely going on. When we walked through the door the first thing that I noticed was Tammy sitting on my parent's couch holding a newborn baby.

As soon as we got inside my mother was standing in the living room with her arms folded over her chest and a look of disgust on her face. Some of the other neighbors were sitting in other chairs in a circle around Tammy and her baby. The men were in the back yard as usual and I found myself in a room full of women who were looking at me as if I were the man of the hour.

As soon as I saw the baby I knew that there was no doubt that the baby was mixed. His skin was still reddish but there was no doubt that the father of this baby was black. Of course that really meant nothing. Tammy only dated black men. He had a wide nose and puffy little lips. Tammy stood up and held the baby out for me to hold.

Everybody in the room started oohing and ahhing as soon as he was in my arms.

CLARK KENT

"Oh my gosh, he looks just like his daddy!" one of the women said excitedly.

"Wow he has your eyes and everything," another woman said as a camera flashed in my face. I stood there holding the baby and felt as though I had been set up.

"Who is that baby, Daddy?" Khalyl asked as he looked at me holding the baby.

"He's your baby brother," one of the women said as if on Que. Khalyl looked at the baby, then back at me inquisitively.

"Daddy, how come he ain't black like me?" he asked. As soon as he said it Tammy's face turned beet red. She gave me mean looks but I tried to ignore it. I looked at Khaly and his light brown skin and then back at the baby. Tammy stood up and grabbed the baby from me. She stormed out of the house and went to stand in the front yard.

I stood there in a room full of women who were all looking at me like I had just done something wrong. My mother gave me a look that told me I had better go and talk to Tammy even though I knew why she was upset. I sent my son to find his Grandpa and went out to hear from Tammy what had upset her. I walked up behind her not quite knowing what to say or do. My heart told me that there was actually a chance that I was the father of her baby, but my mind wandered and told me differently. Her voice echoed in my head, *'It wouldn't be the first time someone was fooled into believing they were the father of a baby that they weren't.'*

Deadbeat Dad

"What did I do? I came here to find out what is going on," I said as I walked up next to her.

"Even he knows, Jason!"

"What are you talking about?" I asked as I turned to face her.

"Even Khalyl knows that he isn't your child. Didn't you hear him ask why our baby isn't black like he is? This is your real son!"

"We were together one time, and since then you have been back with your *baby's daddy.* That's who you need to be talking to, not me."

"I found out that I was pregnant a few weeks after we slept together. I hadn't even had sex with him yet. I didn't want to tell him because I didn't want to make it harder for him to do his time," she said as she covered the baby's face with his blanket.

"Oh and I guess that since he's locked up you figured it would be a good time to play pin the baby on a daddy?" I said as I opened a beer.

"I named my baby after you because I know you are his father! Just like I know that you are not Khalyl's father. If you can't see it that's your own fault but there is no way you are going to lie to my son and tell him that Khalyl's his brother. You are being played! That black bitch has been playing you all along and you know it. This is your real son and you need to choose whether or not you're going to be man enough to accept it or continue living a lie."

CLARK KENT

"Bitch! How dare you come at me like this again? My son has nothing to do with this!"

"He has everything to do with this! Look, you need to decide here and now. Are you going to keep letting some bitch fool you? Or are you going to man up and be a father to your real son?"

"Fuck you bitch! Who in the fuck do you think you are you to try to make me choose your son over my son? I choose Khalyl! Now get the fuck out of here and don't come back, dumb ass bitch! Khalyl is my son and if you don't like it you can suck my dick!" I kicked the garbage can that was sitting at the top of the steps. It fell down the stairs making a loud crash as it went. Tammy ran away carrying her baby crying. I had had enough of this woman questioning the paternity of my son.

She looked over her shoulders as she walked away. There was hate in her eyes. She looked like she was wishing for my death. She stumbled as she looked back at me with tears in her eyes.

"You're going to pay for this, you piece of shit! Mark my words! You will pay for this," she said as she walked away. I turned and walked back inside. The women were huddled up talking but no one said a word to me as I grabbed my son and headed for the back yard.

I never saw Tammy again after that day. She moved away and never even tried to contact me again. All I knew was that she had never changed the boy's name, and that somewhere out there in the world there was a child named Jason Jr. who I would never know; but I never forgot him. The memories of those moments would haunt me for years to come.

Chapter 8
Lovers and Friends

Everything changed when Rhonda got pregnant. From the first day I noticed a change in her. She was literally glowing. It seemed like she had been waiting for the right moment to have a baby and had found it. All she cared about was her new baby.

She bought books about everything from naming a baby, to finding the right college for your child. She wanted to see every store that sold anything that had anything to do with babies. She subscribed to The *Pregnancy* magazine, *Child* magazine and even the *Parenting* magazine.

She was not the woman I knew. The woman I knew ran from love, and vowed to be a player for life. This woman however seemed only concerned with making a family. She promised to get out of the player lifestyle, and be the best wife a man could ever ask for.

I woke up and rolled over to see her lying naked beneath a white sheet. It was spring in Cleveland and as soon as I woke up I could smell the fresh cut grass. It was a Saturday and I had slept in. The sun shined through the window as a breeze made the curtain flap.

The sound of the lawnmower cutting the grass outside had awakened me up from a night of deep dreaming. I looked at the clock and saw that it was just

CLARK KENT

after noon. I pulled myself from the sheets only to find that I was naked as well.

I looked back at the girl lying on the bed; looking like a Goddess. It was Rhonda. I thought about the saying *if it seems too good to be true it probably is.* She was absolutely beautiful. Even with her rounded belly she was sexy.

I thought about all of the things she had given up over the past four months. I had never seen a woman so serious about making a family. She rolled over reaching for the spot where I had laid. When her hands didn't find me she opened her eyes and smiled when she saw me sitting on the edge of the bed.

Just as she began to sit up my phone started ringing. It completely destroyed the moment. As I reached for the phone she lunged forward to grab the phone. The caller I.D. revealed that it was my son's mother. I quickly realized that for the first time in over seven years, I had forgotten to pick my son up.

She was pissed. Rhonda hit the answer button on the phone, and before she could even say *"Hello"* my son's mother was screaming into the phone.

"You; no good son of a bitch! I had appointments today! You were supposed to be here by three o'clock!"

"First of all, hello bitch. This is Rhonda, his fiancée. We just got back into town this morning. He meant to call you yesterday but we were taking care of other more important business. Did he tell you that we're expecting his new baby?"

Deadbeat Dad

The phone went dead and Rhonda rolled over on the bed looking at me with a smirk. She had a devilish look on her face as she propped herself up onto her elbows looking at me. At first I couldn't see what the humor in her eyes was. I had let her cause me to miss my time with my son.

"You owe me, you may not understand right now but I just released you from a spell."

"How in the world could I owe you? If anything you owe me, I'm the one who has to explain all of this!"

"No offense, but that girl has been playing you from the start. She has been pulling your strings for so long that you don't even notice it anymore. It's time for her to learn that she can't play you anymore."

"Look that's my son's mother! What we have has nothing to do with you and me!"

"Exactly! She has nothing to do with us! She had her chance and she blew it! Fuck that bitch, if she can't understand that you have a new woman then she can go to Hell!"

I stood there frozen. I had never had a woman challenge the relationship between me and Khalyl's mother. First Tammy started with the whole thing about Khalyl not being my son, and now Rhonda was telling me that I have been getting played all along. It seemed like something about me and the relationship I had with my son and his mother was setting off alarms with everyone except for me.

The look on her face told me that she meant business. She had decided that she was going to put my son's mother in check. She had determined me to be her property and she wasn't going to let anyone get in her way.

She lunged forward and kissed me. She was smiling and seemed to be on cloud nine. The look in her eyes told me that she was a woman in love. She wrapped her arms around me and jumped into my arms wrapping her legs around my waist.

"Baby, don't be mad. This is our special weekend, and nothing is going to get in the way of us having the best weekend of our lives. I bought you a new outfit, it's in the bathroom. Now get dressed and ready so we can leave already. The plane leaves in three hours."

We had been planning this trip to Atlantic City for months. I had a weeks' worth of vacation from my job and we had all of the money we needed to have a really good weekend in Atlantic City. On top of that I was going with a professional card shark.

I went to the bathroom to see what she had gotten me to wear. Hanging from the shower curtain rod was a short sleeved silk white shirt with some white dress pants. On the counter of the vanity there was a pair of white Stacy Adams shoes with a pair of silk white socks, and a white belt. A white Fedora sat on the opposite side of the sink.

I turned on the shower and let it get hot and steamy before I took my shower. When I got out of the shower I got dressed I walked out to see what Rhonda's reaction would be to the outfit she had bought me. I felt like new money.

"Who are you? My man is in the bathroom getting dressed, and where did you come?"

"I was just in the neighborhood and I was wondering if you would like to accompany me to the casino." I didn't need a response; I knew that she was impressed with the clothes that she had bought me. She was looking at me like was a celebrity. The smile on her face was ear to ear.

She got up and walked towards me with her sexy walk, and before you knew it we were naked in the bed again. She grabbed my face with both hands and stared into my eyes as we made love. As I thrust into her she grabbed my back and let her nails sink into my flesh. She began to moan louder with each stroke. As we climaxed together she collapsed into my arms. I laid her down on the bed and got up in search of my cigarettes and underwear. I stumbled across her purse which had been thrown on the floor in the heat of the moment.

The purse tumbled over and spilled out bundles of cash. I stood naked looking back and forth between her and the bag. I was in shock. I couldn't tell how much money was in the bag but I knew it was a lot. Before I could react she sprung forth from the bed in an attempt to grab the money that had fallen out of the bag. She had the look on her face of a cat with a canary in its mouth.

"I can explain baby, it's not what you think, "she said as she began sweeping the money back into the bag. "This trip is going to be more than a trip. This trip is our trip out. But, its part business too. If we can pull this off

CLARK KENT

we're set for life baby! This is about getting what we deserve. These bitches owe us this!"

"Wait, I don't get it. How did this go from us going on a vacation to you going to pull some kind of heist?"

"Do you remember when we were in Detroit at my friend's wedding party?"

"Yeah, but what does that have to do with this?"

"Do you remember the best man?"

"Yeah the dorky little white guy with the big black girlfriend. What about him?"

"He developed a form of spyware that can give him temporary remote control of a slot machine. He uses these fake players' cards that are encrypted and give him access to the slot machine's computer."

So why can't somebody else do it for him? Why does he want you to do it?"

"Baby there will be ten of us including you. We'll be spread out at different casinos. Everybody will have player's cards for the casinos that they are going to hit. We put big amounts of money into the slot machine and he makes the slot machine's payout up to ten times what we put in. Before they know it we turn $500,000 into five million."

"Wow! I don't know what to say. I mean what if it doesn't work?"

"There will be four other couples working this job. That means that nine of us know that it's going to work. All I need now is for you to believe me. Would I involve us and our baby if it wasn't really worth it?"

Deadbeat Dad

I sat there for a second absorbing what she had just told me. I really didn't want to get involved but it sounded like a fool proof plan. When she had found out that she was pregnant she had promised me that she was getting out of the hustlers life and now she was back at it and trying to get me involved.

"What happened to getting out of the life?"

"It takes money to give up the life Daddy. This is a chance for us to start with a clean slate. After it's all done we walk away with half. That's two and a half million Daddy. I'm putting up $500,000 to make two and a half million. Daddy it's basically free money."

She walked to the closet and grabbed her clothes and then disappeared into the bathroom. I was still in shock. The numbers sounded good but I had no idea that she was into hustles of this magnitude. I knew she was one hell of a hustler, but I just didn't know that she was this deep in the game.

I walked out to the front yard and lit a cigarette. I thought about how much she had resisted me in the beginning. She had flat out told me that she was married to the game. I had never seen a classy woman who was so street smart. She knew how to position herself to be standing where the money landed.

The only way we had gotten so tight was because I had decided that she was out of my league. I told myself that I would just be her friend. I never initiated anything sexual with her. I saw her when she was in town and needed to get away. We were total opposites. I was a father who had a job and a small apartment in the suburbs. She on the other hand was a high steaks hustler, who didn't believe in being caught up in the rat race.

She seemed to be turned off by guys who made advances towards her because those were the kind of men who she used and manipulated. When she saw that I wasn't trying to game her she became more and more available to me.

One night she wanted me to take her to sing Karaoke. By the end of the night we were so drunk that we ended up leaving her car at the bar and catching a cab back to her hotel room. That night she cried in my arms telling me how much she wished she could be a normal girl with a normal life. She broke down and told me how bad she wanted a baby.

That was the first time that we had ever made love. Now it didn't take much more than the mention of sex for us to be jumping into bed. Some days I'd call off of work just to lie in bed with her all day. Things had gotten so serious between us that I was considering letting her meet Khalyl.

The door opened and Rhonda came out looking stunning. She was pulling luggage behind her so I quickly tossed my cigarette and rushed to take the bags from her. She had so many bags that it looked like she was planning to move to Vegas.

"Baby I didn't pack anything yet."

"I took care of that Daddy, we have everything we need. Now let's get going we need to hurry up and get to the airport. The plane leaves in two hours."

Deadbeat Dad

I carried the luggage and tossed it in the back seat of the car. She climbed into the driver's seat and off we went. As we were riding a song by Ludacris and Usher came on the radio. It was called *Lovers and Friends.* As the song played I reflected on how we had become lovers and friends. I had hit the jackpot with this one. I found myself singing along with the radio. Rhonda looked at me and started smiling. We didn't need to say a word. The song had us both thinking the same thing. We were lovers and friends.

Chapter 9
Crash

We sat in an awkward silence at a red light. The song that we had been listening to had gone off. A commercial for a new clothing store was on the radio. The light changed and we began to cross the intersection at 18th and Euclid Avenue. As soon as we were in the intersection, the sound of tires screeching caused us both to look to our left just in time to see the Dodge Caravan plowing into the driver's side of the car.

The impact of the collision spun our car and caused it to start rolling over across the intersection. A car that had been coming from the opposite direction hit us as we flipped into the oncoming traffic. I blacked out.

I was in a coma for eight weeks. When I woke up the first thing that I noticed was that I was in a hospital room. I was confused. I didn't remember the accident or how I could be in the hospital. I looked around the room and saw my parents asleep in chairs next to my bed.

I moved my arm and realized that I was handcuffed to the bed. I tried to sit up and was thrown back down on the bed by the most excruciating pain I had ever felt. Something was wrong with my hips. I screamed out in pain and awoke my parents.

CLARK KENT

The door to the room opened and a huge black man with a suit on came charging in with a gun on his hip, and a badge hanging from a chain on his neck. Alarms started going off and before I knew it the room was filled with doctors, nurses and police officers.

The black man in the suit turned out to be a detective who had been waiting for me to gain consciousness so that he could interrogate me. He tried to push through the crowd but was pushed back as the nurses started rolling my bed out of the door.

"I need to ask him some questions!" he yelled as they pushed me through the door.

"You'll just have to wait officer! This man has to go into surgery stat!"

After hours of surgery I was put into a recovery room. I found out that I had suffered multiple severe injuries. Because I was in a coma the doctors could not perform surgery, so I had been laying in a hospital bed unconscious for eight weeks with a crushed left hip, a dislocated right hip, a gash in my forehead, a bruised heart, bruised lungs and a broken arm.

After surgery when I woke up, everything was different. My memory was coming back and I could remember being in an accident. I remembered seeing a white van coming at us at full speed. I remembered the car flipping over. And then I remembered that Rhonda had been driving.

"Where is Rhonda? I need to see her! Is she okay? Is she in this hospital somewhere too? Please tell me that she's okay. I need to see her now!" My mother came to my bedside and started crying. My father came around to the other side of the bed and grabbed my hand.

"Rhonda didn't make it. I'm sorry son, she died two days after the accident," my dad said as he kissed my hand. My mother started crying and collapsed to the floor. My dad rushed to her side and helped her up.

"What about the baby? She was pregnant with our child!"

"The baby is doing fine. They were able to save her. Her name is Tayla." As my mother said it my heart seemed to explode. I couldn't believe that I would never see Rhonda again. On top of that she had left me the greatest present that a man could ever ask for. She had given me a baby girl. My eyes filled with tears and I cried out loud.

The door opened and Detective Green walked in. He didn't seem moved by the display of emotions going on. He stood next to my father looking at me as though he wanted to charge me with some serious crime.

"Do you remember me? I'm Detective Green. I was here when you came out of your coma."

"What do you want from me? Can't you see this is a bad time?"

"Do you remember the day of your accident?"

"Yeah, why?"

"Do you remember what you were doing before the accident?"

"I was on my way with my girlfriend to the airport. We were going to Atlantic City for a poker tournament."

CLARK KENT

"When we searched the car we found a bag in the trunk carrying over $500,000. Can you explain how you came into so much money?"

"We had emptied out our bank accounts so that she could buy into the tournament."

"So you're telling me that you just happened to have that much money laying around in your bank accounts? What are you some kind of Wall Street executive or something?"

"Look you can check with the banks! I just lost my fiancée. Now if you don't mind we are grieving here. Can you please respect that? The money is legit and it's mine."

"I'll be the judge of that! In the meantime when you get out of here you can pick up your belongings at the station. As for the money, if your story pans out it will be available in a few days. But if I find a single flaw in this story, I will prosecute you to the fullest extent of the law. Do you understand me son?"

"Do what you gotta do, Mr. Officer, but I'll be picking up my luggage as well as my money as soon as I get out of the hospital. Are we clear on that Detective? Like I said, I have nothing to hide the money is legit."

"My condolences, I'll be in touch. In the meantime don't plan any trips beyond the city limits. You are still under investigation." The detective walked to the other side of the bed and took the hand cuffs off of my hand. "Get well soon. I'll be watching you so don't do anything stupid. Good day." The detective walked out of the room and closed the door behind him.

Deadbeat Dad

I collapsed back down onto the bed and started crying again. My mother came over and hugged me. I couldn't believe that she was really gone. I could still smell her perfume in my nose. I remembered seeing her coming out of the bathroom smiling right before we left to go to the airport.

The door opened again and this time it was a beautiful older woman who favored Felicia Rashad. She came in carrying a baby in a car carrier. Behind her two other women who I could tell were Rhonda's sisters came into the room. One of them was carrying a bouquet of flowers.

Rhonda's mother hugged my mother and father and then came to my bed side. As she looked at me her eyes filled with tears. She passed the baby off to my mother and came closer to me.

"I'm so sorry baby; she spoke so highly of you. She told me that the two of you had plans on getting married. She had never spoken about another man the way she spoke of you." My mother had taken the baby out of the carrier and was standing next to Rhonda's mother holding the most beautiful little baby I had ever seen. She handed the baby to me smiling.

"Meet Tayla, your miracle baby," my mother said as she laid the baby in my arms. I reached out and grabbed the baby. She was so tiny that I was almost afraid to hold her. Her eyes looked like miniature versions of Rhonda's. Her skin was pale and her hair was curly and dark.

My eyes filled with tears and I began to weep. I kissed the baby on her head and handed her back to my mother. I still couldn't believe that she had died and that I wasn't even able to go to her funeral. I closed my eyes and my mind replayed seeing the van crashing into us.

A chill went down my spine and I felt like I was in the car flipping again. I could hear Rhonda screaming in terror. Just as she screamed the car landed upside down just in time to be hit by an oncoming car.

When I opened my eyes again the room was empty. The flowers had been put into a vase, and were sitting on the window sill. It had gotten dark outside. I wondered how much time had passed since I had closed my eyes. I reached for the remote to turn the T.V. on. An infomercial was on about knives and kitchenware. I changed the channel and saw that it was three in the morning.

Chapter 10
Nightmares

After flipping through the channels looking for something to watch on TV to no avail, I began to doze off again. I dreamt that I was back at the old heating and cooling warehouse. For some reason I was the only person there and it was dark outside.

I could hear the faint sound of a baby crying but I couldn't tell where it was coming from. I walked past the aisles of air conditioning parts trying to locate the source of the cries. As I walked through the empty warehouse, the cries became screams. I found a staircase leading down to the basement and started walking down them.

As I reached the bottom of the stairs the cries stopped. The silence was eerie to say the least. I started walking through the dark basement not even knowing why. I could see the light shining from under a door up ahead of me. I kept walking towards the door but it seemed like the door was getting further and further away.

Something moving through the darkness in the corner of the room caught my eye. It looked like a baby but it had glowing red eyes and jagged teeth. It was dragging something as it crept along the wall in the darkness. I stood there frozen in fear. It turned and looked at me with those creepy red eyes and began to howl.

CLARK KENT

I turned and started running in the direction of the stairs I had come down but they were gone. I was trapped in the basement with what seemed to be some kind of demon. As I ran I tripped over something and fell to the floor. I stumbled to my feet and tried to run again but when I turned to run the demon was standing in front of me.

It let out a loud howl and threw the bag it had been dragging at me. The bag hit me and knocked me to the floor again. From the bag three heads rolled across the floor. I couldn't tell whose heads they were because they were covered in blood.

The demon charged at me with a large knife in its hand and lunged towards me. I screamed in terror as the demon sliced me across the face. Blood started running down my face. As the demon attacked me I was able to see that it was Jason Jr.

"You left me! You abandoned me! I hate you!" it screamed as it stabbed me again and again. I used the last bit of my strength to grab the demon child but just as I did it disappeared. A chill went down my spine as I looked down and saw the blood that covered my shirt.

I awoke to find myself still in the hospital bed. My hospital gown was soaked from sweat. I couldn't get the image of those red eyes staring at me out of my mind. The TV was turned off and the room was dark.

I sat thinking about Jason Jr. I began to weep thinking about the fact that I had abandoned him. Tammy really had given me no choice in the matter. She was the one who told me to choose between the two children. What kind of father would I have been to choose a baby who I didn't even believe was mine over a child that I loved?

The nightmare had really shaken me up. I jumped as the door to the room opened all of a sudden. A nurse came in and checked my vital signs and asked if everything was alright. I didn't tell her about the nightmare in detail but I did tell her that I had been having bad dreams.

The nurse explained to me that nightmares were common for people who have had severe head trauma. She told me that she had come into the room earlier and could tell that I was having a bad dream. As she talked I couldn't stop thinking about the eyes of the demon child. It had been a very scary dream.

The nurse gave me something to calm my nerves and help me rest. After the nightmare I had just awakened from I really didn't want to go back to sleep. I fought the drowsiness as long as I could but eventually I drifted off to sleep again.

I dreamt that I was back at the scene of the car accident. The car was a mangled wreck that was barely even recognizable. It was upside down and there was blood all over the windshield. As I walked closer I saw my body lying in the road outside of the car. I wasn't moving. Rhonda was inside of the car trapped and screaming for help. Someone came running past me and started trying to free her from the wreckage.

The van that had crashed into us was on fire. The sound of sirens competed with Rhonda's screams as the first responders arrived on the scene. I could see people standing around looking at the cars but no one

CLARK KENT

was paying any attention to my body lying bloody in the street. It was as if No one even cared.

Rhonda was pulled from the wreckage and taken out on a stretcher. One of the firemen walked past me and I tried to get his attention but he didn't hear me. He walked over to my body and nudged me with his foot.

"This one's a goner," he said as he stood over my body looking at me.

Chapter 11
Back to Business

During the time that I had been in the hospital one of the people who were always there for me was Khalyl's mother. She would show up with food for me and sit with me for hours. We would talk about everything. I saw a side of her that I wasn't used to seeing. We had become friends again. I couldn't remember her ever being this nice to me.

Anything that I needed she was there to provide it for me. She brought my son to see me almost every day. Some nights she would even sleep in the chair by my hospital bed. It was a side of her that I hadn't expected to see. When I came home from the hospital she was the person there to pick me up. I was in a wheelchair. She helped me into the car and put the wheelchair in the trunk of the car. When she got into the car she leaned over and kissed my lips.

"I want you to stay at my place for now," she said as she pulled away from the curb. I thought about Khalyl and how much I knew that he would like to see us together as a couple. As we crossed an intersection my body froze and chills went down my spine.

I braced myself thinking that at any moment a car was going to slam into us. I closed my eyes and my mind filled with visions of Rhonda's bloody face. I opened my eyes and saw that we had safely crossed the intersection. My heart was still pounding. I looked over

CLARK KENT

at Khalyl's mother and saw that she hadn't noticed what had just happened.

I sat myself up in my seat and tried to shake it off. The radio was playing a song called; Return of the Mack. I wondered if it would feel like this every time I rode through an intersection. I thought about that beautiful baby girl who would never know her mother. A tear fell from my eye as we pulled up in the parking lot of a restaurant called Lancers.

Lancers was a restaurant/ bar that played live jazz music. It was the place that all of the big time hustlers ate. The parking lot looked like a car show. Khalyl's mother pushed my wheelchair to the door and I could hear the sounds of a local artist named Eddie Backus Jr.

As we walked inside, a beautiful waitress escorted us to a table near the bandstand. She gave us menus and took our drink orders. I ordered a double shot of Hennessy straight, Khalyl's mother ordered her Hennessy with ice.

While we were waiting for our drinks we sat listening to the music and enjoying the atmosphere. I looked over at Khalyl's mother. She was still beautiful after all of these years. Her eyes still had that glow to them and I found myself entranced by their hazel color.

The waitress came back with our drinks and took our order. I ordered a T-bone steak medium well, with wild rice and broccoli with cheese sauce. She ordered a lobster tail and a New York strip steak. The food was delicious. By the time we had finished our food and drinks she was sitting in my lap watching the band. It was our first time ever going out to eat together. When

Deadbeat Dad

Khalyl was born we were both too young to drink let alone go to a bar together.

For the first time in years it seemed like we really could be a couple. She seemed like a totally different person. In reality I knew that we had both changed too much for that. I was really shocked when she paid the tab. After we left the restaurant we went back to her apartment and she told me that she wanted me to stay there for as long as I needed to.

We sat on her balcony talking for a while. My hips had started to hurt again so I took two of my pain pills and went to sleep.

The next morning when I woke up she was gone. There was a note on the nightstand that said she had hair appointments and would be gone for most of the weekend. I rolled over and pulled myself into my wheel chair and rolled out into the living room. She was never one for long goodbyes. I would've actually been more surprised if she had still been there when I woke up

Her apartment was nice. The funny thing was that it didn't really feel lived in. The couches looked like they hadn't been sat on since they had left the show room floor. A glass stand stood in the corner with pictures of her and Khalyl. I rolled over to it and picked up a picture that had been taken on his first birthday. I could still remember taking the picture.

He was wearing his Osh Kosh overalls with a yellow construction hat, and he was holding a toy hammer. The look in his eyes said that he meant business. He was barely walking and he already looked like he was ready to work.

CLARK KENT

I put the picture back on the shelf and went to sit on the balcony. Khalyl's grandmother would be bringing him to see me today and I couldn't wait. As I sat with my eyes closed feeling the warmth of the sun on my face I began to feel alive again. I reached into the pocket of my robe and pulled out the card for the lawyer I had hired. He had asked if I wanted an advance on my settlement and I had told him that I would call him when I was ready. I was definitely ready.

Looking at the business card was like looking at a blank check. My mind danced back and forth with what I would do when I got the money. Out of the corner of my eye I saw a beautiful lady step out onto the balcony across from me.

She lit a cigarette and looked at me smiling. I put the business card back into my pocket and waved at her. She looked to be in her mid to late twenty's. Her hair hung down to her shoulders, and she was very curvy. She stood looking over the waterfront looking lost in thought. When she was done with her cigarette she flicked it over the balcony and waved again smiling as she went back inside.

Apparently she was the next door neighbor, and I had a feeling that I was going to be seeing her again real soon. That feeling turned out to be true. Later that day I was waiting on the elevator when she came walking down the hall from her apartment. She was wearing stretch pants and a sports bra and I could tell that she took very good care of her body.

"You must be Amber's baby's daddy; I'm Mary I live next door," she said as she approached.

Deadbeat Dad

"I'm Jason," I said as I spun my wheelchair around to get a better view.

"She told me about your car accident, but she didn't tell me that you were in a wheelchair. If there is ever anything I can do for you just tap on my door," she said as she pushed the button for the elevator.

"Are you going jogging or something?" I asked

"Not today, I'm just going down to the gym for a quick workout. They have a heated pool down there too. You should check it out, swimming is one of the most important parts of the physical therapy you'll be doing," she said as the elevator door opened.

As she walked into the elevator I found myself staring at her perfect body. On the way down to the lobby she told me that she had worked in a clinic as a physical therapist. When the elevator doors opened she held them open and let me get off first.

I rolled off of the elevator and into the well decorated lobby of the building. Huge glass chandeliers hung from the high ceilings. Large paintings hung on the walls with gold frames. The big glass windows of the lobby looked out over Lake Erie and gave the feeling of standing in front of the ocean. I looked back in time to see Mary walking into exercise room.

I took the business card out of my pocket and looked at it again. I wondered how much money I was going to get from the car accident. I rolled myself towards the entrance to the building. As the automatic doors opened in front of me, I looked back and saw Mary looking at me from the treadmill.

CLARK KENT

Later that night I was sitting on the balcony smoking a cigarette, when I heard a knock at the door. At first I started not to answer the door, but for some reason I found myself rolling across the living room in my wheelchair to answer the door. When I opened the door Mary was smiling and carrying a plate wrapped in tin foil.

"I just came over to offer you some dinner and see how you were doing," she said as she handed me the plate. I could smell the food through the foil. She had definitely gone to extra measures to prepare this meal for me. I found myself almost in a daze looking at her perfect body.

"Well, I hope you like it, I'm having a little get together tomorrow and if you're not doing anything I wanted to invite you over to hang out with us. It'll just be me and a few friends. Besides, I know it's probably lonely over here all by yourself," she said as she turned and began to walk away.

"Well, thank you. I guess I'll see you tomorrow then," I said as I sat the plate in my lap. She looked back over her shoulder and smiled. I could see that she intended for me to see her every curve. She knew that she was eye candy, and it seemed that her flirtatious gestures meant that she also knew that my son's mother and I were not together as a couple.

I opened the foil and saw that she had made a delicious looking meal with baked chicken, potatoes, and asparagus. Everything was perfect. The asparagus had been baked in butter with garlic. The chicken was well seasoned as were the potatoes. When I was done

Deadbeat Dad

eating it all I decided to take the plate back to her and personally thank her.

When she answered the door she was wearing a long black silk robe. I could hear the sound of slow music playing from inside her apartment. She opened the door and motioned for me to come inside. She closed the door and led me into her living room.

Extravagant artwork hung on her walls. The furniture looked expensive and as elegant as the artwork. Her apartment looked like something from a music video. The radio was playing a song by The Isley brothers called Voyage to Atlantis.

"What took you so long?" she asked jokingly as she handed me a glass of Merlot. She sat on the couch across from me with a wine glass and the bottle of Merlot. "Did you enjoy your meal handsome?"

"I did. I couldn't help but coming over to thank you. I haven't had a home cooked meal in a long time. Of course I had to make you wait a little so I wouldn't seem over eager to see you again," I said as I took a sip of the wine. She crossed her legs and the opening of the robe revealed her sexy caramel colored thigh. Looking at her and listening to the slow music seemed to instantly arouse me.

"I knew you'd come over. I saw you checking me out at the gym," she said with a flirtatious smile. I got up out of my wheel chair and sat on the couch next to her. Surprisingly I didn't feel any pain and I as I sat next to her I felt relaxed. She filled my glass and used a remote to dim the lights. That night we made love until I fell asleep. I had made a special new friend.

Chapter 12
Baby Girl

During the time that it took for me to get myself back walking I spent a lot of time with my new daughter Tayla. She was a beautiful baby. Every time that she saw me her eyes lit up like stars in the night.

She was beginning to crawl and make cooing sounds. I bought her a pink bassinette with ruffles on the pillows. A Mobil hung over the top of it with a ballerina that spun to the sounds of lullabies. At night Tayla would lay in the bassinette and stare at the ballerina until her eyes became too heavy to stay open.

She slept through the night pretty much every night. Of course she did have some nights where she wasn't feeling good and cried herself to sleep but she was always a good baby. I kept my alarm set to feed her every few hours. If I didn't force the bottle into her lips I was sure she would be content in her dream land and skip her late night feedings.

It was different having a daughter. I had been used to having a son, but having a daughter was an altogether different thing. Even Khalyl seemed to be mesmerized by her.

On the weekends when he came over he would run right past me looking for his baby sister. He had decided that she belonged to him. Seeing them together

CLARK KENT

reminded me of how much he had grown. He was taking the whole big brother business very seriously.

One day when we were all together enjoying a beautiful spring day at the park I noticed a faraway look in Khalyl's eyes. Normally he would be running around with the other kids at the playground but today he was just sitting at the top of the sliding board. I walked over to him and asked him what was wrong with him.

"Daddy can I ask you something?"

"Of course you can, and you never have to ask if you can ask me a question. What's on your mind man?"

"Why don't we ever see my little brother?" The question caught me off guard. I didn't think he remembered that I had told him he had a little brother. My vision began to blur and I had a ringing sound in my ears. From somewhere in the distance of my mind I could hear someone calling my name I was awakened from my sleep by the sound of a guard yelling at me. I had been dreaming.

"Clark! Get yo ass up you got a visitor," came the voice of the overweight jail guard. I opened my eyes and realized I was sitting in the county jail. I had been pulled over and arrested for non-payment of child support. I had been in jail for three weeks.

I got up from my bunk and walked to the door of my cell. The door opened with a loud clank and bang. As I walked out of the cell I was pushed against the wall and patted down. Once the guard was satisfied with the fact that I wasn't smuggling anything out of jail he led me down the corridor to the visitation room.

Deadbeat Dad

As I walked into the room I immediately saw who my visitor was. My daughter and her grandmother had come to visit me. I walked over to the table and sat down. Tayla was two years old now. She was wearing a burgundy dress and white stockings and shiny black shoes. My little princess came over and gave me a big hug. I picked her up and sat her in my lap.

"I came to pay your bail; they should be letting you go by the time we leave. The reason that we are here is because there is something I need to tell you. My sister in Los Angeles is very sick and I need to be there with her. You are welcome to come with us but if you can't I will make sure you have a way to visit any time that you want to."

"You're moving out there?" I asked.

"Yes, I need to be with my family. I want you to come with us. I know it's asking a lot but I also know how you feel about your daughter." I thought about Khalyl and about how much he would miss me if I moved away. Then I thought about how much I would miss Tayla. There was no way to measure the importance of my relationship with either of them. I decided that I would have to stay in Cleveland and visit my daughter in California when I could.

"Honestly I really appreciate the offer, but I can't just up and leave right now. My son needs me too, not to mention the fact that all of my family is here."

"I understand and I respect that. Any time that you want to visit just let me know and I will get your ticket. We won't be leaving until the end of the month so you will have plenty of time to be with Tayla before we go.

CLARK KENT

Call me when they release you and I will be here to pick you up," she said as she stood up and reached for Tayla.

As they walked out of the visitation room a tear fell from my eye. I couldn't believe that my daughter would be moving away. I told myself that I would be taking the trip to California as often as possible. The guard came over and escorted me back to my cell.

In the three weeks that I had been in the county jail I had made both friends and enemies. Believe it or not the county jail is just about as crazy as the state prison. I walked into the dayroom and headed to the area where the other blacks were seated. The blacks, whites, Latinos, and other races always stayed in their own areas. Everyone stayed with their own kind. Unless the okay had been given; no one violated that rule.

A bald white guy covered in tattoos got up and began walking towards me with a look of sheer hate in his eyes. There had been tension between the whites and black for days. Fights had been breaking out almost every day for at least a week. I had fought the bald guy two days before now, and had really given him a beating. He had just been brought back from the infirmary and I knew he wanted revenge.

As he approached I looked in the direction of the table he was coming from. I looked over to where the blacks were seated and gave a head nod to one of the black men seated at the table. Instantly everyone got up from the black's table and ran in my direction. The bald guy rushed towards me with something in his hand.

Deadbeat Dad

Before he could reach me he was tackled to the ground and the dayroom turned into an open battleground. People got up from different tables and joined in the fight. I ran over and began kicking the bald guy in the head. Another white guy came from behind me and punched me in the back of the head.

As I turned to face him I saw that it was the so-called leader of the white inmates. His eyes were the true reflection of the same hate the bald guy had. He rushed me and threw me to the floor. I quickly rolled him off of me and landed a blow to his nose. The sound of bone crushing was followed by a steady flow of blood from his nose.

An alarm sounded and a voice could be heard on the loud speaker ordering everybody to the ground. I continued punching until he seemed to have passed out. The door to the dayroom opened and a parade of corrections officers in full tactical gear stormed the room. I looked around and saw that there were several other fights still going on. I quickly crawled away from the guy I had been fighting and laid on the floor face down.

The guards cuffed everyone who was still fighting and ushered them out of the room. Those of us who remained were ordered to return to our cells. The few people who remained on the floor in different stages of unconsciousness were picked up and taken out on stretchers. The pod was locked down and we were confined to our cells for the remainder of the evening.

At about 9:00 that night a guard came to the door of my cell and called me out. I was being released. I was

CLARK KENT

taken to a room where a few other inmates were waiting to be released. Right away I recognized one of the black guys from my pod.

"We out brother!" he said as he stood to greet me. A white guy who looked like a member of a motorcycle club stood up and repeated what the first guy said. Now that we were being released it seemed like there was no racial tension. In the pods we didn't even talk to people who weren't from our own races but in the release pen everybody was happy for the same reason. They were going home.

A white guy from the pod I had been in got up and walked over to me. His head and neck were completely covered in tattoos. His arms looked like they would explode if he did any more weightlifting. As he approached other people in the pen moved to the side.

"What's up brother? Thanks for looking out for me. If you ever need anything be sure to look me up," he said as he grabbed me in a bear hug.

"Man we all good, I was just watching out for my celly," I said as I patted him on the back. I had helped him to study for his G.E.D. at night after lock down. During the day we never spoke to each other out in the pod. If the heads of our races knew that we were friends and that he was learning to read and do math from a black man, they would have killed us both.

During my time in the county jail I had learned a lot about people. Though we were all in there for more or less the same things we were all very different. In jail there are no fine lines. The boundaries are as present

Deadbeat Dad

as the bars on the cells. However in the release pen everybody is happy.

An hour later I walked out of the county jail and into the cool fall air in Cleveland. As I walked past the big black pipes that are supposed to be some kind of a sculpture I looked back at the building I was walking away from. It almost felt as if the building were staring at me.

As I continued walking I heard the sound of a familiar female voice calling my name. I turned around and saw three women standing outside of a grey Cadillac. It was Mary and some of her friends with her. One of the girls was a Latina girl who I had never seen before. She was a petite girl with perky breast and a big smile. The other girl was Angel, a short voluptuous white girl who was one of Mary's closest friends with benefits.

Mary was a different kind of woman. She was a boss and she knew it. She seemed to always have an entourage no matter where she went. She also was known to have more than enough hired guns on her payroll to protect her high profile lifestyle. It didn't take long before I noticed the cars parked at either end of the block. They were her personal bodyguards.

Mary had been a one hit wonder during the early eighties and used the money she made to build her drug empire. She was the crack Queen Pen. The word on the streets was that she was worth millions. I always thought she was worth at least a billion. Either way she was from a whole different tax bracket and she loved her some Jason.

CLARK KENT

Angel broke free from the group and ran at me full speed. She jumped into my arms and started kissing my face. I lowered her to the ground and she held on even after her feet had touched the ground.

"Have you met Star?" she asked as she turned back to face the Cadillac. Star was the Latina girl and she looked happy to meet me. She stepped forward extending her hand. I grabbed her hand and kissed it. Just as I did Mary stepped in between us.

"Yes this is my boo thang. She is off limits baby!" she said as she came over to hug me. As I hugged her I looked over her shoulder at Star and saw her looking at me like I was a bag of popcorn in a movie theater. The sound of a car horn caused everybody to turn around and look in the direction of the street.

As soon as I saw the black Lincoln Continental pull to the curb I knew it was Rhonda's mother. She was also known for her flamboyant lifestyle. She owned at least three cars and never drove. Her driver was an older man named James Foxx. James was more of a multi-purpose bodyguard than a driver.

Rhonda's mother always reminded me of Felicia Rashaad. She was a beautiful older black woman whose presence demanded respect. She was educated, elegant and financially well off. She was also single. People often questioned whether we were intimate because she was very territorial about me.

James got out of the car wearing one of his signature suites. He was wearing a royal blue pinstripe suite with a pair of matching blue alligator skinned shoes. As he walked around the car he lowered his Ray-Ban glassed and reached out for me smiling.

"What kind of bird can't fly?" he asked as he walked over to me. Mary rolled her eyes as he gave me a hug. She was never a fan of anyone who took the spot light off of her.

"Daddy we gotta go! Time is money," Mary said as she turned and started walking to the Cadillac. The other two girls opened the passenger side doors of the Cadillac and motioned for me to follow. James laughed out loud in a way meant as an insult.

"Man c'mon we got real business to tend to," he said as he put his hand on my shoulder and basically guided me to the Lincoln. I turned and saw Mary looking at us with an angry look on her face. Before she could say anything her phone started ringing. She flipped it open and started talking. Over her shoulder she flipped me the "call me" sign and got into the Cadillac.

When I walked over to the Lincoln I saw that Tayla was in her car seat fast asleep. I thought about the fact that they were going to be moving to California and felt instant sadness. She was as much of a part of me as Khalyl was. I had gotten very used to spending time with her and watching her grow. Soon she would be living thousands of miles away.

Chapter 13
Star Struck

Mr. Fox was the man who knew everything about everyone. His limousines did the foot work for Cleveland's elite class. He often drove for some of the most influential people in the city. As we pulled away from the county jail he laughed and stuck up his middle finger to one of Mary's bodyguards who was parked at the end of the block.

"She's trouble. She is one evil bitch Jason. My advice would be to stay out of her circle," he said as we turned onto Euclid Avenue. I looked at him and wondered how he knew her. She was definitely a baller but I didn't think he would be someone to run in the same circles as her. Ms. Williams was in a completely different class than Mary.

"Do you know about what happened between her and your son's mother?"

"I didn't even think they knew each other like that," I said as I sat looking out at the city.

"Oh they definitely know each other. They're damn near arch rivals these days. I was working for Mary when I met Amber. Mary was running girls back and forth between here and Chicago. Amber had just finished cosmetology school and she did all of the girl's hair. Mary liked Amber but Amber wasn't into that kind of thing.

CLARK KENT

Mary poured it on her thick too. When Mary got busted the Feds tried to make Amber flip on Mary but she wouldn't do it. They knew Amber had information that could help them lock Mary away for a long time.

Mary ended up beating the case. She almost caused me to lose my business. When the Feds couldn't get to Mary through Amber they sent the dogs my way. I had everybody from the IRS to the FBI knocking on my door. I had to let go of the account.

Mary thought that the reason Amber hadn't flipped on her was because Amber liked her. It turned out that that wasn't the case. Amber didn't flip on Mary because she knew how much power Mary had in the streets.

One day Mary tried to corner Amber and Amber stabbed the shit out of her. Mary never told the police who had stabbed her. Since then they have stayed as far away from each other as possible."

"They live right next door to each other though."

"Amber hasn't stayed in that apartment for quite some time. Didn't you see how unlived in that apartment is? Mary rented that apartment for Amber when she was trying to get her." I thought about the first time I had gone to Amber's apartment. I remembered how the furniture looked like it had never been used.

I remembered how Mary had known who I was and that she knew I had been staying in Amber's apartment alone. She had suckered me in. She had been playing a game from the start. The dinners, the parties with her girls, and the expensive shopping sprees were all in an

Deadbeat Dad

attempt to get even with Amber. I had fallen for it hook, line, and sinker.

I wondered if Amber knew about Mary and me. I was sure that Mary had made it known to her that we had been together. Maybe that was the reason Amber stayed away from the apartment. Amber was no dummy; she had probably known what would happen when she first took me to her apartment. I had been served up like a sacrificial lamb. Two women had used me against each other but I knew exactly how to turn the tables on them.

It occurred to me that Mary had used me to make Amber jealous, but Amber had used me to keep Mary off of her back. I decided that I was going to steal Mary's girl and make them both jealous. I was going to steal Mary's star.

We pulled into the driveway in front of Ms. William's house. When he turned off the car Mr. Fox turned to me with a serious look on his face. He was the kind of guy whose opinion mattered. He was the man behind the scenes who had a hand in everything.

"Listen son, you're caught up in one hell of a mess. Whatever you do, remember that these women are well connected. They can get rid of you faster than ashes from a cigarette. My advice would be to just pack it up and move to California with Ms. Williams.

Consider it a second chance if you will. Ms. Williams is a very powerful lady too. Believe me she knows what's going on out here. She only wants to see you do what's right. You have babies to think about, what I'm saying is choose your next move wisely," he said as he opened his door to get out of the car.

Ms. William's house was beautiful. It had big white pillars and white shutters on the windows. Two golden statues of lions sat on either side of the door. The golden hardware made the doors look like they belonged on a mansion. It was almost hard to believe that a girl like Rhonda had grown up in a house of this magnitude.

When the door opened Ms. Williams smiled and led us into a large living room with furniture that appeared to be antique. The legs of the couches and chaise were gold with what looked like large paws at the bottoms. Over the fireplace was a painting of Ms. Williams standing with a man and three little girls.

I could tell that the girls were Rhonda and her sisters. The man standing next to Ms. Williams looked to be a white man. He was wearing a black suite with a red ascot around his neck. As I looked closer I could tell from his facial features that he was mixed. His skin was very light colored but he had a wide nose and high cheek bones. He looked like a jazz musician.

"That was her father. We met when I was in law school at Case Western. He thought he was God's gift to women," Ms. Williams said as she walked into the room. "You remind of him. I'll bet that was what my daughter loved about you. Her father and I were from two different worlds.

He was a smooth talking lady's man, and I was a naive little school girl. When he was killed it broke Rhonda's heart. She cried every night for years. Jason I don't want that history to be repeated. I don't want Tayla to have to go through what her mother went through. I really wish you would come with us to California.

These streets of Cleveland are vicious. These girls out here playing mind games will get you killed. I have been a lawyer for over twenty years, and I have represented too many young people who simply made the wrong decisions."

Mr. Fox came into the room and told us that Tayla was in her crib sleeping. He bragged about his special abilities in being Uncle J and then we all went to the dining room to eat the dinner that Ms. Williams had prepared for us.

She disappeared into the kitchen as we sat ourselves at the table. Everything about her house said class. From a speaker hidden in some corner Johnny Hartman sang to the sound of John Coltrane playing his saxophone. *"Let the years come and go, I'll still feel the glow that time cannot fade... When I hear that lovely autumn serenade."*

Ms. Williams returned carrying a casserole dish with oven mitts on. She sat it on the table and went back into the kitchen. Mr. Fox got up and went to the kitchen to help her with the food. My phone started ringing so I checked the caller ID.

It was Mary. I pressed the ignore button and put my phone back into my pocket. Two minutes later my phone chimed again telling me that I had a text message. I decided not to check it because I knew the message was from Mary.

CLARK KENT

Mr. Fox and Ms. Williams came back into the room with the rest of the meal. Looking at them made me wonder if they were secretly involved. She always laughed at his jokes, and he was always extremely kind to her. Whatever was going on they were extremely close.

After dinner I went up to kiss Tayla goodnight. My eyes filled with tears thinking of her being gone to California. I kissed her on her forehead careful not to wake her and left. On my way out I thanked Ms. Williams for inviting me and gave her a hug. Mr. Fox got up to walk me to the door.

I needed to get back on the scene. My time in the county had taken a toll on me both mentally and physically. I had to get things back together. I was headed to Club 66 on Hough Avenue.

Club 66 was your average whole in the wall bar, but secretly it was where all of the hustlers hung out. It was also the place where I knew I would find Mary. She was like a fixture in the place.

She usually had a hand in on every hustle in town. People showed me respect just because I had been introduced by her. As I walked up to the door a big black guy appeared in the doorway.

"What's up Tiny?" I said as I walked past him into the bar. Tiny was about 6'4 and weighed at least 300lbs. He was the door man. If he didn't know you it was a sure bet that you wouldn't be going inside.

Deadbeat Dad

"What's up little man," he said as he moved aside to let me in. The bar was dark and the smell of cigarettes was strong. Through the Smokey haze I spotted Mary sitting at the end of the bar on her phone. Angel and Star were seated on either side of her.

As I looked around I saw all of the big time players from almost every hood. Sitting at the bar by the door was Hos and his right hand man Kert. Standing next to Kert was a guy by the name of Old Man. He was a Hough heights original known as a ruthless killer.

As I made my way to the back of the bar I heard my name being called. I turned around and saw big bank Hank and the twins; Mikey, and Ikey. Hank was wearing a mink hooded jacket with a big gold chain around his neck. Mikey and Ikey were wearing matching Gucci sweaters and Kangol hats.

They were big time players from Cleveland Heights. They were known throughout the city for always being associated with big money. Hank walked over and gave me a hug. We knew each other from grade school. We had always been good friends.

"I heard you were in the slammer my nigga," Hank said as he signaled for a waitress to bring us drinks.

"It was just some bullshit that needed to be taken care of," I said as we walked over to the table they were sitting at. As I sat down I noticed Star staring at me from the bar. She winked and blew me a kiss as she sipped her drink. Mary was on the phone in what looked like an important conversation.

CLARK KENT

"I heard yo' dumb ass was in the county acting like a damn fool," Mikey said as I sat down. "Fool you know I had yo' back though. I got people everywhere lil nigga. I heard you were giving it to them peckerwoods too! Nigga's been talking fool," he said as he passed me a blunt. I reached into my pocket to get a lighter, but before I could a waitress walked up with our drinks. After she sat the drinks down on the table she pulled a lighter from her bosom and lit the blunt for me.

"Shit man, I was just trying to keep myself alive. Shit was real in there," I said as the waitress walked away smiling at us.

"Shut up fool, that was just time out. The pen is where shit is real. Little nigga gets a spankin' and try to act like he been on punishment. Drink up fool, welcome home."

Angel walked over and sat on my lap. She smelled as good as she looked. She was Mary's girl but we had gotten to know each other at one of Mary's parties. Her big breasts were right in my face and I was beginning to get excited. She put her lips close to my ear and told me that Mary was mad at me. She kissed my cheek and got up. She looked back over her shoulder and winked as she walked back to the bar.

"This nigga must got some mean ass game," Ikey said as we watched her walk away. He had been on the phone when I sat down and probably hadn't even noticed me. I owed him some money from before I had gotten locked up.

"What's up with them chips though my nigga?" he said as he downed his drink.

Deadbeat Dad

"I'm working on it baby, I just got out today," I said as I stood to follow Angel.

"Work smarter and harder then and get me my ends nigga!" he said as I began to walk away from the table. He and I only dealt with each other because of Mikey and Hank. We had never really liked each other.

He was a spoiled rich kid who grew up in the suburbs and I had moved up through the ranks in the streets. He was also known to have a crush on Amber. I threw up a two fingered peace sign and walked away. I had just gotten out of jail and I wasn't in the mood to be phony or be around people who I was in debt to.

Before I could get to the bar I felt a hand on my shoulder. I turned around to see Dave an old friend of mine from Wade Park smiling at me. I hadn't seen him since we were kids. We had grown up as best friends but he had gone to prison for shooting up a dice game when we were thirteen years old.

We chatted for a few minutes reminiscing on old times, but my focus was on Star the whole time. She had been my main reason for coming to Club 66. Dave and I exchanged contact information and then I proceeded to the bar to say hello to Mary and her girls. I wanted to get to know Star, she was the forbidden fruit and I was "Star" struck.

As soon as I walked over to them Mary flipped me off. She was still mad that I hadn't left the county jail with her. I signaled for the bartender and ordered a drink. The first thing that I noticed was that Star couldn't take her eyes off of me.

CLARK KENT

"Evening ladies," I said as I sat on a bar stool next to them.

"You're a real piece of work; I had something I needed you to do. I wouldn't have come all the way down there to pick you up if it wasn't important," Mary said. The bartender came over with two shot glasses of Hennessey.

"I only wanted one, boss," I said as I reached for my drink.

"The other one is from the lady in blue over there," he said as he pointed down the bar. I looked down the bar and saw my ex-girlfriend Angie smiling at me. I raised my glass and winked at her as I downed my shot. The Hennessey burned as it went down but it didn't bother me at all.

"Hey, I'll be right back I need to say hello to an old friend," I told Mary as I got up. I walked over and couldn't help but to notice how beautiful Angie looked in her blue dress. It had been years since I had last seen her, but she hadn't aged a day. Her reddish- auburn hair rested on her shoulders and her lipstick was an almost perfect color match as her hair.

"Well hello handsome," she said smiling as I sat next to her.

"Hey there pretty lady. Long time no see," I replied.

"I'm here with a friend so I won't keep you long. Besides I see that you're busy over there with your little girlfriends," she said as she downed her drink.

Deadbeat Dad

"I'm actually here on business. It's definitely nice to see you though," I told her.

"My number hasn't changed; you should try to remember it. Maybe we can hook up some time for old time sake," she said as she kissed my cheek. I stood up and before I could turn around I found myself face to face with the biggest black dude I could imagine.

He was at least 6'5 and had to have weighed at least 300 pounds. As I stood, the first thing that I noticed was how angry he was. He must've been in love with Angie and I could see that he completely blamed me for what he had seen.

My first instinct was almost to run but after a second of thought I decided that there was nowhere for me to go. I had to face this humongous beast of a man head on. I stood up and the first words to escape my mouth surprised even me.

"Excuse me big man, but I need to hit the restroom!"

"What in the fuck is going on over here?" he yelled before I could make my way past him.

"Baby!!! What is the problem, this is Jason. He's the one I told you about!" yelled Angie as she jumped in between us. Before I knew it the club seemed to stand at a pause. I had a reputation, and there were plenty of people who were willing to stand in my defense but the big guy must've been just as connected as I was.

Mikey and Hank came and stood behind me and I knew that they were both heavily armed. Apparently Angie's boyfriend was someone who they had beef with and they were eager for a confrontation. Mary and her

CLARK KENT

girls walked up behind Angie and for a second I thought that they were about to jump her.

"Let's go baby I don't have time for this bullshit," the big man said as he turned around and headed for the door. As he moved for the exit three other men who had been watching from a nearby table got up and followed him out. One of them turned around and pointed his fingers like an imaginary gun and shot an imaginary bullet at us.

I went back and sat with Mary and Star, and Angel to finish my drink and get to know Star. At the time I didn't know it but over the course of the next three years Star and I would be bringing two beautiful daughters into the world and living on the other side of the country in Tucson, Arizona.

Chapter 14
The Girls

Sitting on my park bench I came to the realization that as much as I had wanted to be a good father I had basically failed in doing so. I have been everything from father of the year to an abusive husband. I have tried six times to be a family man and six times I have failed.

As a woman walked by pushing a double stroller with twins, I thought about when my daughters; Jayla and Jazzmin were babies. I had just relocated to Tucson and once again I had decided to try again to be the father that I wanted to be.

Star and I had been together for a year and eight months when Jayla was born. During the time that we had been together I had started seeing my other children less and less. Khalyl was older now and the fact that we had found out that I wasn't his biological father hadn't really helped our relationship.

I hadn't seen Jason Jr. since he was eleven months old. Tammy had gotten her wish to have a mixed baby and not have to deal with the father. I never forgot him though especially since I was reminded every payday when I saw the child support taken from my checks.

Tayla was living in California with her grandmother and it wasn't very often that I could get out to California for visits although we kept contact via phone

CLARK KENT

occasionally. She was growing up. Our conversations were usually short.

I would ask how she was doing and hear her normal response *"Fine."* I would ask how school was going even though I knew her response would be *"Good."* I would make small talk before eventually telling her that *"I loved her and missed her and that I would see her soon."*

I spent my afternoons taking Jayla for walks in her stroller. She loved going for walks. I watched as her face showed fascination with the trees and the birds. She waved at every person who walked by. She was my princess. Her mother and I however fought like cats and dogs.

We really didn't have much in common other than our attraction to each other. It almost seemed like the only time that we got along was when we were between the sheets. We argued about just about everything.

She liked 2Pac and I was more of a Biggie fan. She liked going out and I preferred staying at home. She liked going on expensive shopping sprees while I was more concerned with trying to save money. The list went on and on.

I often found myself putting Jayla in her stroller and going anywhere just to be away from home. I used to take her to the zoo, to the Children's museum, or the library and sometimes we would just go for a ride on the bus.

She reminded me a lot of her sister Tayla. She was a happy baby. She hardly ever cried. I found myself

Deadbeat Dad

reliving a lot of the memories that I had from when Tayla was a baby. Sometimes it even felt like déjà vu.

I had decided that I was going to be with Jayla whether Star and I got along or not. It turned out to be a bigger challenge than I thought it would be. Our fights got worse and worse. They also got more frequent.

It was both of our faults because we both did things to piss each other off. Some days it would be me hitting her and some days it was her getting her payback. We were a toxic combination, but we always ended the fights with steamy passionate sex.

I was almost ready to quit when I found out that we were expecting another baby. I decided once again that being there as a father was more important than letting an argument cause me to leave.

I found out that we were going to be having another baby girl. Her name was going to be Jazzmin Monai. I was the happiest man in the world. Now I was going to have two little princesses to spend my days with.

They were twenty two months apart. Jayla was walking and beginning to talk. Jayla was convinced that Jazzmin was her baby. She wanted to help feed Jazzmin, she wanted to try to hold Jazzmin, and she refused to be separated from Jazzmin.

As they got older it seemed that they were the perfect playmates for each other. Jayla always shared everything with Jazzmin. I usually just bought two of everything because I knew they would want the same things. Sometimes I even dressed them in the same clothes and people actually asked if they were twins.

CLARK KENT

I had upgraded to a double stroller. I found myself taking them to the same places I had taken the other babies. My favorite place to take them was to the Tucson zoo. It wasn't a particularly big zoo, but it had a great assortment of animals and the girls loved being there.

That was about the time when Star decided to pursue a career in the world of exotic dancing. It started out fairly innocent. She took a job as a waitress in a strip club called T.D's. It was an upscale club on the east side of Tucson.

I often found myself going to the club just to watch her work. She would walk by and bring me drinks while I watched the girls on the stage. She had a special talent for charming the customers as she served them drinks. It didn't take long before she herself was on the stage and giving lap dances.

To keep me from being jealous she would send other girls to give me lap dances. I became a regular in the club. I started to drink excessively. The nights of me being in the club drinking gave way for the many fights that Star and I had.

One night she dropped the girls off at her mother's house while I was passed out on the couch. I woke up and saw that they were gone and I already knew that something was wrong. I tried to call her phone and it went straight to voicemail. I called the white girl and she told me that Star had confronted her at the club the bouncers had broken up the fight and kicked star out of the club.

Deadbeat Dad

When she came into the house without the girls I knew it was bad. She had a bottle of Jack Daniels that she had just about finished. She put the bottle on the table and opened her purse. Whatever she was about to do was I was sure I deserved it. This was my fault I had been cheating on her. Until now she hadn't been able to prove it but now I was busted.

She walked into the living room and turned the radio on and then came to stand in the doorway of the kitchen. She lit a cigarette and walked back to her purse. She reminded me once again what would happen if I cheated on her. She had told me that if she found out that I really was cheating she was going to kill me.

I stood by the sink looking at her. She was laughing but I could tell there was nothing funny. "It's bad enough that I found but what made it worse was that I had to find out through gossip. You couldn't even be man enough to tell me," she said as she reached into her purse and pulled out a gun.

She was furious. We were in our kitchen and there was no way for me to get past her. When she started going off it was too late for me to do anything. She was blocking the doorway and she had my gun in her hand screaming at me. I knew that the gun was loaded and I knew that she meant business.

"How could you fuck that gringo bitch?" she said as she cocked the hammer back on my .38 special. "I work my ass off to keep this house together. I do everything that you need, and that's the thanks I get?" Her hands were shaking and her eyes were filled with tears. She squeezed the trigger and a bullet whizzed right pat my head.

The wall behind me crumbled in a blast as the bullet crashed through it. She came closer to me. She was still screaming but I could no longer hear what she was saying. My ears were ringing. I looked at the barrel of the gun and saw that she still had two more bullets. She pointed the gun at me again and pulled back the hammer.

"Is this what you want?" she said as she pointed the gun at my chest. I immediately dove across the room and tackled her. As we fell to the floor the gun went off again. When we landed on the floor I snatched the gun from her and threw it across the room. I was about to start hitting her when I looked down and saw that I had been shot in the stomach.

I fell to the floor and the pain started to shoot up my body. I was bleeding a lot and it burned like hell. Star jumped up and ran to my side. She put her hand over the bullet wound and called 911.

"Oh God no! Baby I'm sorry," she screamed as she put pressure on the bullet wound. I couldn't believe she had shot me. My vision started to blur and eventually I passed out. When I woke up I was in a hospital bed and Star was asleep in the chair by my bed. The bullet had gone straight through my side.

She had told the police that I had accidentally shot myself putting the gun away. They must've believed her because they never came to question me afterward. When I got out of the hospital we knew that we could no longer stay together. As much as we wanted to try again we knew that it was over. We had to split up for the sake of the kids as well as for safety's sake.

On top of that we had found out that the white girl was saying she was pregnant. She was claiming that I had gotten her pregnant before I had gotten shot. She had taken a restraining order out on Star and as a result Star was fired from the club.

Sitting on my park bench listening to the sounds of the children play I decided that it was time to stop making excuses and find my way back into my children's lives. The memories that I have of the times we have shared are precious jewels that I store in my heart.

I got up and began to walk away from the park. I had children who needed me and I needed to figure out what I would have to do to get back into their lives. I told myself that I would call each one of my babies and tell them that though I may have at times been a deadbeat dad that I had never stopped loving them.

About the Author

Clark Kent is a fictional author who writes about urban life and situations. His stories reflect the feelings and emotions that are felt when life happens. As an avid reader himself Clark enjoys the trill of an exciting story. The characters that he uses are all fictional and based on the lives of just about all of us.

He began writing short stories at an early age, and has always been a good story teller. His first book Yellow was published in 2014 followed shortly after by Yellow Vegas, and Yellow Cleveland (the man of peace).

YELLOW

CLARK KENT

Deadbeat Dad

CLARK KENT

www.ingramcontent.com/pod-product-compliance
Lightning Source LLC
Chambersburg PA
CBHW071516040426
42444CB00008B/1669